ORYX
SCIENCE
BIBLIOGRAPHIES

Volume 9

Animal Experimentation and Animal Rights

Compiled by Ruth Friedman
David A. Tyckoson, Series Editor

ORYX PRESS
1987

The rare Arabian Oryx is believed to have inspired the myth of the unicorn. This desert antelope became virtually extinct in the early 1960s. At that time several groups of international conservationists arranged to have 9 animals sent to the Phoenix Zoo to be the nucleus of a captive breeding herd. Today the Oryx population is over 400, and herds have been returned to reserves in Israel, Jordan, and Oman.

Published by The Oryx Press
2214 North Central at Encanto
Phoenix, AZ 85004-1483

Published simultaneously in Canada

Printed and Bound in the United States of America

Library of Congress Cataloging-in-Publication Data

Animal experimentation and animal rights.

(Oryx science bibliographies ; v. 9)
Includes index.
1. Animals, Treatment of—Bibliography. 2. Animal experimentation—Bibliography. I. Friedman, Ruth. II. Series.
Z7164.C45A55   1987   [HV4708]   016.179′3   86-43115
ISBN 0-89774-377-6

Table of Contents

Oryx Science Bibliographies
David A. Tyckoson, Series Editor

About the Series

The Oryx Science Bibliographies are a new series of bibliographies designed to bring you the most recent references on the current issues in the sciences. Each issue will provide between 200-300 fully annotated references along with a "Research Review" covering the history and state of the art of the topic being covered. These bibliographies are intended to provide the student or researcher with an effective introduction to the hot topics in the sciences. Each bibliography also contains a number of special features, such as:

Evaluative Selection: The bibliographer reviews each article to ensure that only the most valuable references are included. The bibliography does not strive to be comprehensive but to include only the most important items on the topic.

Fully Annotated: All of the references are annotated, providing a useful summary of the source material for the user.

Readily Available Materials: All references chosen for inclusion are available at most libraries throughout the United States and Canada. Obscure sources that are difficult to obtain are usually avoided.

Highly Current: The bibliography strives to include the most recent materials to keep it as up to date as possible. References from as recently as the last six months before publication may be found in all issues.

Key Articles Highlighted: The most important articles in each bibliography are highlighted in **boldface** so that the user interested in only a few materials can key in to those that are the most useful.

Research Review: Each issue contains a research review describing the state of the art of the subject being covered.

1

Undergraduate Level: Only materials that are written at the undergraduate student level are chosen. Neither highly technical nor extremely general articles are included.

English Language Only: Only English language materials are included.

Research Review: Animal Experimentation

Animal Experimentation in the Context of the Animal Rights Movement

The movement to control or abolish animal experimentation is one segment of the overall animal rights movement, an effort which is again gaining momentum. This movement comprises a wide variety of organizations and philosophies, but most members of the animal rights movement object to the intentional and/or unintentional mistreatment of animals for the "advancement" of humanity. Some proponents of animal welfare object to the modern farming methods by which poultry, calves, and other animals are raised. Others are concerned with the treatment of animals in exhibitions such as zoos and circuses. Some animal rights groups advocate vegetarianism and others object to the slaughter of animals in order to obtain parts of their bodies for commercial products such as furs or ivory. Hunting is considered by some as an inhumane sport. This bibliography will deal primarily with the use of animals in scientific research, but the arguments used by animal rights activists are very similar when discussing any of these issues.

The Animal Experimentation Controversy

Controversy regarding animal experimentation has continued and increased ever since antivivisectionists first challenged scientists in the nineteenth century. Initial arguments against animal research were based on the obvious pain and suffering of animals in response to laboratory procedures. The scientific community responded by presenting the numerous and significant biomedical advances attributed, in great measure, to animal experimentation. Some researchers believed, based upon the theory of evolution or the Bible, that humans have absolute dominion over animals and thus may use them as we please. Today, animal welfare advocates primarily refer to the insignificance of most research, the needless duplication of experimentation, the use of too many animals, and the unnecessary pain and distress to which many laboratory animals are subjected. Research projects should be judged on relevance and the costs of not doing particular experiments should be considered as

well.   Research groups counter these arguments by
claiming that scientific advancement is not possible
without continued animal experimentation, that anesthesia
is used whenever possible in order to minimize pain and
suffering, that there is no way to know in advance which
specific experiments will lead to significant results,
and that duplication of research experiments are an
essential part of the scientific process.

Philosophical and Ethical Arguments

In the last ten years, philosophical and ethical
arguments have become important forces for limiting or
eliminating the use of animals.   The advocates of
"humane" treatment hold that although humans are entitled
to experiment on animals for their own purposes, they
should do so without causing unnecessary pain or
distress.   The "utilitarian" view, described by
philosopher Peter Singer, weighs animals' pain and
distress against the benefits derived from their use.
Since little benefit is produced compared to the amount
of pain inflicted in many experiments, animal
experimentation should be severely restricted.   Equality
is based on an equal consideration of interests which are
limited only by "sentience," the ability to feel or sense
something.   Since animals feel pain, their suffering is   *quote*
of equal value to that of humans.   Primate
experimentation raises ethical problems for the very
reasons that nonhuman primates are used: they are
evolutionarily close to humans and some nonhuman primates
have abilities exceeding those of young or debilitated
humans.   The philosopher Tom Regan takes what he calls
the "rights view":   individuals, regardless of species,
equally possess inherent value or rights.   All
individuals are entitled, therefore, to equal
consideration.   For humans to treat nonhuman animals as
if they were of lesser value constitutes "speciesism,"
analogous to racism or sexism.   For those who adhere to
Regan's philosophy, it is absolutely wrong to conduct any
animal research whatsoever.

Early History of Animal Experimentation

Experimentation on animals dates back to at least
500 B.C. when Greek scientists began dissecting dead
animals in order to understand their internal body
structure.   By the third century B.C., in Alexandria,
living animals were being dissected, and function as well

4

as anatomy became the object of interest and speculation. The thirteenth century saw the dissection of human bodies for anatomical study and in the 1600s it was argued that experimentation on animals could add to the scientific knowledge of human subjects.

The seventeenth and eighteenth centuries brought a great increase in scientific activity resulting in the recognition of animal experimentation by educated people other than scientists. By the latter half of the 1800s, experimental research and the introduction of anesthesia made possible the systematic study of physiology followed by other biomedical sciences, all dependent upon animal experimentation. The word "vivisection" at first meaning the dissection of living animals without anesthesia, was later used for all animal experimentation, including that performed under anesthesia.

The Antivivisection Movement and the "Cruelty to Animals Act"

Opposition to animal experimentation began to be voiced following the spread of animal experimentation in Europe. However, the antivivisection movement, the organized opposition to experiments on living animals, was started in Great Britain in the 1870s. Led by Frances Power Cobbe, anti-vivisectionists opposed all animal experimentation, drug, bacteria administration, dissection and surgery. In response to the antivivisection movement, the British "Cruelty to Animals Act" of 1876, still in force today, was enacted. The law, which requires registration of experimental laboratories, licensure of experimenters, certification for particular experiments, record keeping and reporting, had the effect of drastically decreasing the number of experiments performed. This movement continues to be active in England, where the latest government report on the issue was presented in 1985.

United States Federal Legislation

In the United States, the American Association for the Prevention of Cruelty to Animals, the American Anti-Vivisection Society, and the American Humane Society all became active in the late 1800s. Federal antivivisection legislation, opposed by scientists and physicians, was introduced but failed to gain passage at the same time that major biomedical advances led to decreased mortality

5

rates and a commitment to continued experimentation. In the 1940s and 1950s, state humane societies fought to keep animals from pounds out of research laboratories. The "Laboratory Animal Welfare Act," whose name was subsequently changed to the "Animal Welfare Act of 1966," provided for the regulation of the transportation of dogs, cats, and certain other animals destined for use in laboratories and elsewhere. The Act was amended in 1970 to provide for humane standards in the handling, care, treatment, and transportation of animals. The "Animal Welfare Act Amendments of 1970" also gave the Secretary of Agriculture the responsibility to investigate and inspect animal facilities and to confiscate or destroy animals found to be suffering. The "Animal Welfare Act Amendments of 1976" increased protections and prohibited the sale or use of stolen animals.

In 1985, the United States government, reacting to pressure from animal rights advocates, promulgated two laws which further regulated animal experimentation and encouraged decreased animal use. "Subtitle F - Animal Welfare," of the "Food Security Act of 1985," amends the "Animal Welfare Act" by specifying minimum standards for humane treatment of animals and directing researchers to minimize pain and distress as well as to consider alternative research procedures. This law provides for government inspections and reports, and for the establishment of institutional animal care committees to inspect facilities and review research practices. The "Health Research Extension Act of 1985" requires the National Institutes of Health to establish guidelines for the proper care and treatment of animals and for NIH grantees to comply with those guidelines. Researchers must train personnel to use humane techniques and methods that limit animal use and distress. The responsibilities of animal care committees are also specified in this new law.

The Animal Experiments

Millions of laboratory animals are used in research each year. They provide products of direct benefit to humans, such as insulin or heart valves. They are used to produce vaccines and antibodies and for the diagnosis of diseases in both humans and animals. Many experiments are used to screen substances such as potential new cosmetics for hazardous side effects. Animals are the subjects of biomedical and psychological research projects, are used to develop new medical technologies,

6

to test new drugs, and as model systems to emulate human diseases and disorders. Many animals are used in basic research which adds to the store of general scientific knowledge. Educational institutions, including high schools, colleges, and schools for health professionals, make use of animals in their teaching programs.

Perhaps the most controversial experimental use of animals is in the toxicity testing of such substances such as cosmetics, cleaning agents, and other commercial products. Two tests in particular have come under attack. The LD50 test, used by industry to satisfy government testing requirements, requires that large numbers of animals be force fed large amounts of potentially toxic substances until half of the animals die and the survivors have also been made sick. In the Draize eye irritancy test, concentrated substances such as shampoos are dropped into the eyes of rabbits whose eyelids are fastened open. Both of these tests are useful in determining the harmful and toxic effects of new products, but both also can cause severe pain and death for the animals used in the experiments. Animal rights activists claim that tests such as these cause undue pain and suffering in the test animals, but scientists believe that these tests are essential in preventing unforeseen negative reactions of those same products in humans.

Animal Welfare Advocates and the Animal Liberation Movement

Toxicity tests and other applied and basic research experiments have been the targets of many animal welfare advocates, including some of the scientists themselves. In addition to the standard ethical, philosophical, and pain and suffering arguments, some of their concerns are also based on "good science." Much animal research is needlessly repetitive and may have inconclusive results. Animals that are kept under laboratory conditions rather than in their normal habitats may not respond normally when subjected to experimentation. Variables such as food, temperature, lighting, noise, and socialization affect experimental results and reliability. It is also both expensive and time consuming to conduct a large number of experiments on many animals.

In recent years, animal welfare advocates have been well organized, vocal and, at times, militant in their activities. They have held demonstrations at important research institutions such as the American Museum of Natural History and the National Institutes of Health to end objectionable research involving animals. They have infiltrated laboratories, photographed conditions, destroyed files, and "liberated" research animals. They have brought suit against individual scientists and government agencies and have succeeded in having experiments and research funds suspended in some cases. In England, a radical group caused chaos by falsely claiming to have poisoned candy produced by a company which funds animal research on tooth decay. Animal welfare advocates have also had their views extensively published in a wide range of media.

Alternatives to Traditional Animal Experimentation

A major emphasis of the animal welfare movement, and an idea that has been embraced by industry, government and scientists alike, has been the search for and utilization of alternatives to traditional animal experimentation. Research into alternatives has been guided by principles known as the "three R's:" Refinement of experimental techniques to cause less pain and suffering; Replacement of animals with nonanimal procedures; and Reduction in the number of animals used in experiments. The Federal Office of Technology Assessment has produced a major study on alternatives, the National Institutes of Health now requires its grantees to consider alternatives to proposed research involving animals, and the Food and Drug Administration no longer requires the traditional LD50 test. Industry has also responded by funding centers at Johns Hopkins and Rockefeller Universities where research on alternative techniques is currently in progress.

Although scientists state that the total replacement of animals in laboratory experiments is not possible and that animals and human subjects continue to be necessary for final testing, alternatives have been and continue to be developed which are contributing to a decrease in animal use. A modified LD50 test uses fewer animals for shorter time periods while progressive symptoms of toxicity are recorded. A modified Draize test utilizes lower concentrations of chemicals, regular eye washes, and the collection of sloughed cells, providing quantitative measures of irritancy. Scientists are also developing in-vitro substitutes to replace whole animal toxicity testing. In addition to the many cell and tissue culture studies, researchers are using membranes from chick eggs, human placentas, and corneas from the eyes of animals already at slaughter houses.) The Ames test, in which bacteria are used for initial testing of toxic chemicals, has led to decreased animal use even as the amount of chemical screening has increased. Recombinant DNA technology is providing substances such as insulin without the use of animals. Physical and chemical assays are being performed using sophisticated techniques such as gas-liquid chromatography and mass spectroscopy. Computer modelling and mathematical analysis provide other promising research avenues.

The Future of Animal Experimentation

Both the animal welfare and scientific communities are interested in reducing the numbers of animals used in laboratory experiments: the animal rights advocates on the basis of philosophical and ethical arguments and the scientists on the basis of a reduction of the cost and speed of conducting research. As alternative methods are developed, they will slowly replace traditional animal experiments. Additional state, federal, and international regulation will help to prevent the unnecessary exploitation of animal species. Most scientists believe that animal experimentation will always remain an essential part of scientific research, but all concerned parties will work to make sure that it is only used when it is the most appropriate experimental technique.

Ruth Friedman
Drew University
December 1986

Bibliographies

1.   Magel, Charles R.   A Bibliography on Animal Rights and Related Matters. Washington, DC: University Press of America, 1981. 602p.

   This unannotated, nonselective bibliography of over 3000 English language items includes almost 450 citations to items published on animal experimentation since the 1800s. Other subjects include animals and human nature, religion, ethics, eating animals, hunting, domestication, spectator   entertainment,   environmental   issues, organizations, and cookbooks.

2.   Magel, Charles R.   "An Updated Bibliography."   In Salt, Henry S. Animals' Rights Considered in Relation to Social Progress. Clarks Summit, PA: Society for Animal Rights, 1980. (originally published in 1892.) pp. 171-218.

   A bibliography on animal rights containing many citations on animal experimentation.

3.   U.S. Department of Health and Human Services. National   Library   of   Medicine.   Reference   Services Division. Laboratory Animal Welfare, compiled by Fritz P. Gluckstein.   Bethesda, MD: National Library of Medicine. (Specialized Bibliography Series. SBS numbers 1984-1, 1985-1, 1986-1.) Superintendent of Documents numbers HE 20,3614/6:1984-1, HE 20.3614/6:1985-1, and HE 20.3614/6:986-1.

   A series of annotated bibliographies describing journal articles, books and monographs from the academic, medical and veterinary literature on laboratory animal welfare.

Animal Experimentation Issues: General and Comprehensive Reports

4.   Allen, Don W.   "The Rights of Nonhuman Animals and World Public Order: A Global Assessment." New York Law School Law Review, v. 28, 1983, pp. 377-429.
     This article on animal rights includes discussion of the economic aspects of animal experimentation, animal activists' success in lobbying government and industry to fund research into alternatives, strategies used by the "deprivors and the defenders" of animal rights, and national and international laws and agreements designed to protect animals.

5.   Archibald, J., J. Ditchfield and H. C. Roswell, eds. The Contribution of Laboratory Animal Science to the Welfare of Man and Animals. Stuttgart; New York: Gustav Fischer Verlag, 1985.   450p.   (8th Symposium of the International Council for Laboratory Animal Science (ICLAS)/ Canadian Association for Laboratory Animal Science (CALAS), Vancouver, 31, July - 5, August, 1983.)
     Issues discussed in this recent symposium include the interrelationships of humans and animals, training and education for laboratory animal science, the animal rights movement, and ethical questions.   Specific experimental studies are reported as well.   Animal experimentation is necessary, but unnecessary suffering and waste of research animals is to be minimized.

6.   Begley, Sharon, Mary Hager and Susan Katz. "Liberation in the Labs; Animal-Rights Groups are Gaining Clout and Respect." Newsweek, v. 104, August 27, 1984, pp. 66-67.
     Philosophically, scientists range from those who don't take critics of animal experimentation seriously to those who use animals only because there are no other available models as close to humans.   Animal rights groups have members who are against any animal experimentation whatsoever.   Specific animal tests, currently available alternatives and the movement to develop new alternatives are discussed.

7.   Dodds, **W.** Jean **and** Barbara F. Orlans, eds.
<u>Scientific Perspectives on Animal Welfare</u>.   New York:
Academic Press, 1982.   131p.   (Proceedings of the First
Conference on Scientific Perspectives in Animal Welfare,
held Nov. 11-13, 1981, in Chevy Chase, Md., sponsored by
the Scientists Center for Animal Welfare.)
     Ninety scientists, proponents of the use of animals
in research, met to discuss and recommend "responsible"
use of animals.   They addressed the responsibilities of
individual investigators, institutions, funding agencies
and the editorial process for the humane treatment of
animals.   Scientists   should   participate   in   the
determination of public policy.

8.   Dresser, Rebecca.   **"Research on Animals:** Values,
Politics, and Regulatory Reform."   <u>Southern California
Law Review</u>, v. 58, July 1985, pp. 1147-1201.
     Explores the history and politics of the controversy
over animal experimentation, the nature and scope of
current animal use, current laws, philosophical arguments
on the moral status of laboratory animals, proposals for
reforming research practices, ethical review committees
for regulating animal research, and potential standards
and procedures for regulating experimentation on animals.

9.   "The Ethics of Animal Testing."   <u>The Economist</u>, v.
291, April 7, 1984, p. 87.
     Andrew N. Rowan's <u>Of Mice, Models, and Men</u> (no. 20)
is the source of this report on British statistics on
animal use, pain and emotion in animals, and tests which
cause   animals   discomfort   and   are   of   questionable
validity.   Alternatives   to   reduce   animal   use   and
suffering are suggested.

10.   Fox, Michael Allen.   <u>The Case for Animal
Experimentation: An Evolutionary and Ethical Perspective</u>.
Berkeley: University of California Press, 1986.   262p.
     Animals should be used for human purposes.   Human
welfare is more important than animal welfare because
humans are more important than animals.   Evolution,
ethics, past and current research, and alternatives to
animal experimentation are discussed.

11.   Fox, Michael W.   "Laboratory Animals."   In Fox, Michael W.   Returning to Eden: Animal Rights and Human Responsibility. New York: Viking Press, 1980.   pp. 105-135.
     Statistics on laboratory animal use, the conditions under which the animal subjects are held, the validity of animal experiments, toxicity studies, testing of carcinogens and other potential biohazards, pain and suffering, needless repetition, science fair projects, and humane alternatives are some of the issues covered. Although it is important to experiment on animals in order to save lives and treat disease in animals and humans, research projects should be judged on credibility and relevance and demonstrate reverence for all life.

12.   Goodman, Walter.   "Of Mice, Monkeys and Men." Newsweek, v. 100, August 9, 1982, p. 61.
     Explains the views of research scientists and extreme antivivisectionists: those who justify experimentation on animals by its prospective benefit to humans and those who see no excuse if the animal involved is not to benefit. Peter Singer's concept of speciesism is also explained.

13.   Herscovici, Alan.   "Animals in Research and on Factory Farms." In Herscovici, Alan. Second Nature: The Animal-Rights Controversy.   Canadian Broadcasting Corp Enterprises, 1985. pp. 171-181.
     Reviews the positions of major animal rights spokespersons and details statistics of laboratory animal use, specific tests and experiments. Some scientists believe that in order to decide whether to do a specific experiment, one must evaluate the cost of not doing that experiment.

14.   Holden, Constance.   "A Pivotal Year for Lab Animal Welfare."   Science, v. 232, April 11, 1986, pp. 147-150.
     Recent U.S. legislative and regulatory activity and the specific activities of animal rights groups are reviewed. Describes cases in which the numbers of animals in use have been curtailed, the effect of the current economic situation facing academic and private industry, and the continued development of new laboratory and information methodologies to reduce the use of animals in research.

14

15. Jones, Peter M. "Experimenting on Animals: What Limits?" Senior Scholastic, v. 113, May 1, 1981, pp. 12-14.
      Research scientists feel that experimentation on animals is necessary while others, including some researchers themselves, question whether it is necessary to hurt or kill animals. The reasoning on both sides, traditional tests, and newer alternatives are described.

16. Leepson, Marc. "Animal Rights." Editorial Research Reports, v. 2, August 8, 1980, pp. 563-580.
      Speciesism, experimentation, factory farming, and vegetarianism are all covered in this review of animal rights. Statistics on research animal use, arguments for and against animal experimentation, the controversy surrounding testing of cosmetic products, and the possibility of using alternatives to animals in research are presented.

17. "Man or Mouse." Scientific American, v. 250, May 1984, pp. 62-66.
      The activities of animal welfare groups and scientists who have organized to educate the public on the value of animal research are described. Federal and state regulatory legislation, both currently in force and proposed, is also presented.

18. Paton, William. Man and Mouse: Animals in Medical Research. Oxford; New York: Oxford University Press, 1984. 174p.
      A thorough and detailed overview of the types of animals and types of experiments; ethical issues; benefits of animal experimentation; issues of pain, suffering and death; alternatives; and similarities and differences between man and animals. Scientists should only conduct experiments that must be "good science" and in which suffering is minimized so that future benefit can be realized.

19. Rollin, Bernard E. "The Use and Abuse of Animals in Research." In Rollin, Bernard E. Animal Rights and Human Morality. Buffalo, NY: Prometheus Books, 1981. pp. 89-148.
Surveys the experimental uses of animals in research, testing, safety evaluation, education, and product extraction. "Utilitarian" and "rights" arguments are used in recommending amelioration of animal suffering by improving or eliminating certain experiments, proposing new regulatory legislation, sacrificing certain new products, and changing science education.

20. Rowan, Andrew N. Of Mice, Models, and Men: A Critical Evaluation of Animal Research, Albany: State University of New York Press, 1984. 323p.
This comprehensive book on the use of animals in scientific research reviews the subject from its history to modern day alternatives, covering attitudes, assumptions and morals; primate and pound animal research; pain and suffering; and toxicity testing. An extensive bibliography documents the scholarly research and includes many of the important authors and sources in the field of animal experimentation.

21. Rowan, Andrew N. and Bernard E. Rollin. "Animal Research--For and Against: A Philosophical, Social, and Historical Perspective." Perspectives in Biology and Medicine. v. 27, Autumn 1983, pp. 1-17.
A review of the history of animal research and the opposition movement, U.S. legislation and legislative proposals, and the current animal welfare climate. The differences between biomedical scientists and animal welfare advocates are really only differences in emphasis and the time frame for resolution of the conflict.

22. Ryder, Richard D. Victims of Science, 2d rev. ed. London: National Anti-Vivisection Society, 1983. 180p.
Describes specific experiments whereby agents such as weed-killers, pesticides, cosmetics, neurological weapons, and electric shock are tested on animals. The unpleasant conditions under which lab animals are kept are detailed and it is suggested that many animal experiments are invalidly applied to human situations. Alternative techniques are proposed and the philosophy of speciesism is defined and discussed.

23.   Sechzer, Jeri A., ed.   The Role of Animals in Biomedical Research. New York: New York Academy of Sciences, 1983. 229p. (Annals of the New York Academy of Sciences, v. 406.)
    This scholarly work describes animal research methodology and discusses when it is necessary to use animals, when alternatives are feasible, and the ethical and public policy issues involved in both U.S. and international research.

24.   Singer, Peter.   "Tools for Research...Or What the Public Doesn't Know It Is Paying For."   In Singer, Peter. Animal Liberation: A New Ethics for Our Treatment of Animals. New York: A New York Review Book, distributed by Random House, 1975. pp. 29-95.
    A philosopher who is a major force in the animal rights movement describes specific experiments to which animals are subjected in the laboratory.   The similarities between animals and humans are discussed and the parallel between speciesism and racism is proposed. Scientists don't look for alternatives because they don't care enough about animals and because they are led by economic concerns.   Private citizens and students can protest and reduce the levels of animal experimentation.

25.   Sperlinger, David, ed. Animals in Research: New Perspectives in Animal Experimentation. Chichester; New York: John Wiley & Sons, 1981. 373p.
    Presents a broad coverage of animal experimentation with sections devoted to social, political and legal issues; scientific and medical use of animals; alternatives; the fallacy of animal experimentation in psychology; and the advancement of knowledge and ethical problems.

26.   Stevens, Christine.   "Animal Torture in Corporate Dungeons". Business and Society Review, no. 49, Spring 1984, pp. 39-43.
    Advocates a reduction in the "massive amounts of purposeless suffering of test animals" and describes specific painful and lethal tests, pending legislation and lawsuits, tests conducted in a fraudulent manner, and some actions that national and international agencies should take.

27.   U.S. National Institutes of Health. Office for Protection from Research Risks. <u>National Symposium on Imperatives In Research Animal Use: Scientific Needs and Animal Welfare, April 11-12, 1984</u>.   Washington, DC: Government Printing Office, 1985.   Superintendent of Documents number   HE20.3002:An5/7.

    This symposium reports medical advances made possible by animal research. Responsible use of animals is advocated, varying perspectives (ethical, activist, veterinary, legislative, voluntary) are presented, and alternative research models and control of pain are discussed.

28.   Zola, Judith C. et al.   "Animal Experimentation: Issues for the 1980s."   <u>Science, Technology & Human Values</u>, v. 9, Spring 1984, pp. 40-50.
    Describes the history of animal experimentation, relevant international legislation, the controversy between those who would abolish and those who would reform   animal   research,   proposed   U.S.   regulatory legislation, and ideas for resolution of the conflict.

Animal Experimentation: Philosophy, Ethics, Morality

29.   Andes, Bob. "Ghosts." <u>New Scientist</u>, v. 101, March 15, 1984, p. 32.
        A poem that dramatizes the difficult choices involved in the animal experimentation issue by using ghost imagery: innocent animals who suffer and die and innocent humans who suffer and die.

30.   "Arrogance of the Species?" <u>The Economist</u>, v. 286, March 19, 1983, p. 20.
        After describing Peter Singer's concept of speciesism, whereby humans practice moral favoritism towards their own kind, this opinion article rationalizes our special status while calling for improvement in our treatment of experimental animals.

31.   Bateson, Patrick. "When to Experiment on Animals." <u>New Scientist</u>, v. 109, February 20, 1986, pp. 30-32.
        Opposing sides may become too polarized to compromise on pending British animal welfare legislation. A model is suggested by which research proposals would be evaluated by weighing the quality of research, certainty of medical benefit, and degree of animal suffering.

32.   Beardsley, Tim. "Laboratory Animals: The Case for the Defence." <u>Nature</u>, v. 304, August 4, 1983, p. 388.
        Scientists, meeting at the invitation of science writers, asserted that important research and testing could proceed only with experiments on living animals.

33.   Bowd, Alan D. "Ethics and Animal Experimentation." <u>American Psychologist</u>, v. 35, February 1980, pp. 224-225.
        Argues against psychologists' justifications for their treatment of animals: that animal interests may be sacrificed to satisfy human interests and that animal interests may be disregarded in order to advance scientific knowledge. Alternative techniques must be implemented to replace or reduce the use of animals.

34.   Boyce, John R., with Christopher Lutes.   "Animal Rights: How Much Pain Is a Cure Worth?"   Christianity Today, v. 29, September 6, 1985, pp. 35-38.
     Presents a Christian view of animal rights that states that although God has given humans dominion over animals and experiments may be conducted for human benefit, intentional cruelty cannot be justified. Justification for cosmetics, weapons testing, and certain repetitive educational experiments are questioned.

35.   Burghardt, Gordon M. and Harold A. Herzog, Jr. "Beyond Conspecifics: Is Brer Rabbit Our Brother?" BioScience, v. 30, November 1980, pp. 763-768.
     An essay with an extensive bibliography reviewing the ethical and philosophical arguments surrounding consideration of humans' relations with other species. Examples are drawn from the animal experimentation controversy as well as issues involving hunting, fishing, use of animals for clothing, farming methods, and vegetarianism.

36.   Cohen, Bennett J.   "Animal Rights and Animal Experimentation."   In Basson, Marc D.   Rights and Responsibilities in Modern Medicine.   New York: Alan R. Liss, 1981.   pp. 85-92.
     Animal experimentation is necessary to answer "properly posed scientific quesions," but requires the assurance that "humane considerations" be applied. Humane treatment is discussed in terms of proper experimental design, laboratory housing, and medical and surgical procedures.

37.   "Do Laboratory Animals Have Rights?"   Nature, v. 302, March 24, 1983, p. 287.
     Describes the philosophy of a leading animal rights philosopher, Peter Singer, and then refutes Singer's arguments by citing the views of the scientific community. Three letters of reaction, pro and con, are included on page 649.

38.   Fox, M. W.   "On the Use of Animals in Research."
American Psychologist, v. 37, May 1982, pp. 598-599.
     A refutation of the article by Gallistel (no. 39)
arguing against scientists who consider human suffering,
much of it self-induced, to be more important than
experimentally induced animal suffering.   Research
avenues in paleontology, ethology, or anthropology can be
used as non-destructive alternatives for scientists to
pursue.

39.   Gallistel, C. R.   "Bell, Magendie, and the Proposals
to Restrict the Use of Animals in Neurobehavioral
Research." _American Psychologist_, v. 36, April 1981, pp.
357-360.
     Recounts episodes from the history of neuroscience
to demonstrate that: 1) although animal experimentation
causes pain and distress, science cannot progress without
it, and 2) although most research animals, in retrospect,
are seen to have suffered in vain, it is impossible to
predict which experiments will yield meaningful data.

40.   Gendin, Sidney.   "The Animal Experiments
Controversy." _American Psychologist_, v. 37, May 1982,
pp. 595-596.
     Contends that Gallistel (no. 39) misrepresents "The
Research Modernization Act" bill, overlooks the
controversial issues concerning establishment of humane
conditions for experimentation, and presents no arguments
for the claim that experiments on living animals are
indispensible to scientific progress.

41.   Hoff, Christina.   "Immoral and Moral Uses of
Animals." _New England Journal of Medicine_, v. 302,
January 10, 1980, pp. 115-118.
     An editorial reviewing arguments indicating the
dominance of humans over animals. Animals may be used in
painful experiments that are to yield vital benefits for
humans or other animals, but should not be used when
"substantial" benefits are not expected.

42. Jamieson, Dale and Tom Regan. "The Use of Animals in Science." In Regan, Tom and Donald VanDeVeer. And Justice for All: New Introductory Essays in Ethics and Public Policy. Totowa, NJ: Rowman and Allanheld, 1983. pp. 169-196.
   Philosophical arguments and criticisms are presented in order to demonstrate the various positions favoring or opposing all uses of animals for scientific purposes or allowing that some animals may sometimes be used for some of these purposes. The accompanying notes and bibliography provide extensive source material on animal experimentation and the broader animal rights issues.

43. Kelly, Jeffrey A. "Disagreement with Gallistel: The Need for Increased Scrutiny of Animal Research." American Psychologist, v. 37, May 1982, pp. 596-598.
   In response to the article by Gallistel (no. 39), the cost associated with supporting every proposed research study would be pain endured pointlessly by many animals.

44. King, Frederick A. "Animals in Research: The Case for Experimentation." Psychology Today, v. 18, September 1984, pp. 56-58.
   The director of the Yerkes Regional Primate Research Center refutes animal rights activists' charges of cruelty to animals. The standards and mechanisms of control which protect animals are described and a case is made for continued animal research, particularly in the area of psychology.

45. Maddox, John. "Laboratory Animals: Huxley Attacks Animal Rightists." Nature, v. 306, December 8, 1983, p. 527.
   Sir Andrew Huxley, President of Britain's Royal Society, defended laboratory animal experiments and complained of the disruptive activities of individuals from animal rights organizations. He supported the continuation, in future British legislation, of the "pain condition," which requires that animals suffering pain which is likely to endure should be killed immediately after an experiment.

46. "Monkey Business." The Economist, v. 293, December 8, 1984, pp. 12-14.
     This editorial endorses legislative means rather than terrorist tactics for control of experimentation on animals. Legislation should reflect considerations of scientific purpose, animal pain and suffering, and alternative experimental techniques.

47. Regan, Tom. "Animal Experimentation: First Thoughts." In Regan, Tom. All That Dwell Therein; Animal Rights and Environmental Ethics. Berkeley: University of California Press, 1982. pp. 61-74.
     Philosophical arguments are used to justify total abolition or significant reduction of the use of animals in research. Advocates preventing cruelty, increasing kindness, utilitarianism (placing value on consequences), and the basic moral rights of animals "not to be treated merely as a means to human ends."

48. Regan, Tom. "Animal Rights and Animal Experimentation." In Basson, Marc D. Rights and Responsibilities in Modern Medicine. New York: Alan R. Liss, 1981, pp. 69-83.
     Anything which feels pain has a right not to be hurt. Concepts germaine to the animal experimentation controversy are: "speciesism," a prejudice against members of species other than one's own; the view that only rational beings have moral rights; the "sentience" view that individuals who can experience pain and pleasure have moral rights; and according of legal as well as moral rights to animals.

49. Regan, Tom. "The Dog in the Lifeboat: An Exchange." New York Review of Books, v. 32, April 25, 1985, pp. 56-57.
     A reply to Peter Singer (no. 55), explaining the theoretical foundation of the animal rights movement. His willingness to sacrifice a dog in an overloaded lifeboat is not inconsistent with his opposition to the harmful use of animals in science.

50.   Rosenfeld, Albert.   "Animal Rights vs. Human Health." Science '81, v. 2, June 1981, pp. 18-22.
    Safeguards currently in use in the United States protect animal subjects of medical research while the search for alternative research techniques continues. Humans do act as if they have dominion over nonhuman animals, demonstrating Peter Singer's idea of speciesism.

51.   Ross, Michael W.   "The Ethics of Experiments on Higher Animals."   In Keehn, J. D.   The Ethics of Psychological Research.   Oxford; New York: Pergamon Press, 1982. pp. 51-60.
    Discusses the concepts of suffering, animals as rational beings, similarities between animal subjects and scientists, and the ethics of the methods used by scientists. Researchers should follow "the 5 R's" of ethical treatment and improved scientific method: replacement, reduction, refinement, rationale, and responsibility.

52.   Ryder, Richard D.   "Speciesism in the Laboratory." In Singer, Peter.   In Defense of Animals.   New York: Basil Blackwell, 1985, pp. 77-88.
    Focuses on concern for the victim: it is wrong to kill and cause pain or suffering. Statistics indicate the size of the problem, examples of specific laboratory experiments demonstrate its scope, and alternative research techniques are suggested. Animal welfare advocates use methods such as political pressure, sabotage of laboratories, freeing of animals, and attacks on personal property to combat speciesism in the laboratory.

53.   Salt, Henry S. "Experimental Torture." In Animal Rights: Considered in Relation to Social Progress. Clarks Summit, PA: Society for Animal Rights, 1980 reprint, pp. 90-103. [originally published in 1892]
    Although the language is Victorian English, the concepts in this reprinted edition could come from today's animal rights literature: that animals are "automata" devoid of spirit, character, and individuality; humans are prejudiced against lower animals; humans regard animals as incapable of possessing rights; and vivisection is justified by its utility. We must present "consistent opposition to cruelty in every form and phase."

24

54.   Singer, Peter.   "Animal Experimentation.   II.
Philosophical   Perspectives."   In Reich, Warren   T.
Encyclopedia of Bioethics.   New York: The Free Press,
1978. v. 1, pp. 79-83.
     Describes the philosophical cases both for and
against experimenting on animals, the positions of those
who would completely abolish such experimentation and
others who advocate reform, and comments on the moral
status of animals.

55.   Singer, Peter.   "The Dog in the Lifeboat: An
Exchange: Peter Singer Replies."   New York Review of
Books, v. 32, April 2, 1985, p. 57.
     In this letter, Singer again disagrees with Regan's
lifeboat argument (no. 49) but agrees wholeheartedly with
Regan's attack on the use of animals as research tools.

56.   Singer, Peter.   "Ten Years of Animal Liberation."
New York Review of Books, v. 31,   January 17, 1985, pp.
46-52.
     Singer, in this major bibliographic essay, reviews
ten recent books on animal rights, comparing all of the
authors' views to his own.   Tracing the rise of the
animal liberation movement in America, he explains the
authors' philosophies and criticizes extensively.

57.   Swan, Alma.   "Exhortation to Scientists."   New
Scientist, v. 101, March 15, 1984, p. 32.
     A reaction to a Physiological Society document which
encourages experimentation without regard for relevance
or suffering.   Society members should object to being
associated with such insensitive and irresponsible views.

58.   Tannenbaum, Jerrold and Andrew N. Rowan.
"Rethinking the Morality of Animal Research."   Hastings
Center Report, v. 15, October 1985, pp. 32-43.
     A review of the major ethical positions which strive
to determine the moral status of animals; the concepts of
pain, suffering and pleasure as applied to animals; and
the benefits, to humans and other animals, of animal
research. An extensive bibliography is provided.

59.   "This Is What You Thought About...Medical
Experiments on Animals." Glamour, v. 79, December 1981,
p. 59.
        In this survey of Glamour readers, almost two-thirds
of those who answered felt that testing and medical
research on animals should not be continued. Of those
who preferred scientific use of some animals and not
others, 82% chose rats.

History of Animal Experimentation

60.   French, Richard D.   "Animal Experimentation: I. Historical Aspects." In Reich, Warren T. Encyclopedia of Bioethics. New York: The Free Press, 1978. v. 1. pp. 75-79.
    The history of animal experimentation is presented beginning in classical Greek times, through the rise of opposition and the antivivisection movement, and ending with relevant legislation in Great Britain, the United States, and elsewhere.

61.   Ritvo, Harriet.   "Plus Ca Change: Antivivisection Then and Now." Science, Technology and Human Values, v. 9, Spring 1984, pp. 57-66. Reprinted in BioScience, v. 34, November 1984, pp. 626-633.
    This report on a 1983 conference on research with animals begins with an extensive history of the animal protection movement and ends with the sentiment that all current legislative efforts favor those who would allow research on animals without inflicting suffering. "Antivivisection" will flourish as long as there continue to be those who argue that humans have no right to exploit other species for their own benefit.

62.   Sechzer, Jeri A.   "Historical Issues Concerning Animal Experimentation in the United States." In Keehn, J. D. The Ethics of Psychological Research. Oxford; New York: Pergamon Press, 1981. pp. 13-17. (Social Science and Medicine, v. 15F, no. 1.)
    Compares the history of the United States movement to control animal experimentation to its predecessor movement in Britain. In reaction to activity by animal protection groups, U.S. scientists are moving toward self-regulation to reduce the numbers of animals used, reduce unnecessary duplication of experiments, and minimize pain and distress.

U.S. Laws Governing Animal Experimentation

63.   "Animal Welfare Act Amendments of 1976."   (Public Law 94-279).   United States Statutes at Large, v. 90, April 22, 1976, pp. 417-423.
   The purpose of this law is to increase the protection afforded animals in transit; to assure humane care and treatment of animals intended for use in research facilities, exhibition, or as pets; and to prevent the sale or use of animals which have been stolen.

64.   "Animal Welfare Act Amendments of 1970."   (Public Law 91-579).   United States Statutes at Large, v. 84, December 24, 1970, pp. 1560-1565.
   Directs the Secretary of Agriculture to promulgate humane standards for handling, care, treatment and transportation of animals for research and other purposes. The Secretary must also investigate or inspect animal facilities and has the power to confiscate or destroy, in a humane manner, animals found to be suffering.

65.   "Animal Welfare Act of 1966."   (Public Law 89-544). United States Statutes at Large, v. 80, August 23, 1966, pp. 350-353.
   This law authorizes the Secretary of Agriculture to regulate the transportation of dogs, cats, and certain other animals intended to be used for research and other purposes.

66.   "Food Security Act of 1985."   (Public Law 99-198). United States Statutes at Large, v. 99, December 23, 1985, pp. 1354-1660.
   Sections 1751-1759, "Subtitle F--Animal Welfare," effective December 1986, amend the Animal Welfare Act. Researchers must employ specified minimum standards for humane treatment of animals; minimize pain and distress; consider alternative procedures; limit major operations performed on an animal; report annually and submit to inspection; establish institutional animal care committees to inspect facilities and review research practices; and file reports for the Department of Agriculture and other federal funding agencies.

67.   "Health Research Extension Act of 1985."   (Public Law 99-158).   United States Statutes at Large, v. 99, November 20, 1985, pp. 820-886.

This law directs the Secretary of Health and Human Services, acting through the Director of NIH, to: establish guidelines for the proper care and treatment of research animals; require animal care committees at each NIH funded facility; specify the responsibilities of those committees; require that potential grantees assure NIH of compliance with its guidelines; require potential grantees to train personnel in humane animal maintenance, experimentation, and the availablilty and use of methods that limit animal use and distress.   If the provisions are not met and grantees do not correct deficiencies, the Director of NIH must suspend or revoke research grants.

U.S. Federal Legislation, Regulations, and Guidelines

68. "Animals and Animal Products: Animal Welfare." <u>U.S. Code of Federal Regulations</u>, Title 9, Subchapter A, Parts 1,2, and 3.

Rules and regulations pertaining to the Animal Welfare Act, as amended, are contained in this section of the <u>Code of Federal Regulations</u> (CFR).

69. Beardsley, Tim. "Laboratory Animals: US Protection Act Approved." <u>Nature</u>, v. 319, January 2, 1986, p. 7.

Reports on the provisions of the Improved Standards for Laboratory Animals Act bill which was supported by scientists' organizations and the American Society for the Protection of Animals.

70. Beardsley, Tim. "U.S. Laboratory Animals: NIH Watchdog Committees." <u>Nature</u>, v. 315, May 23, 1985, p. 267.

The Department of Health and Human Services has issued guidelines for animal use committees which review research programs and inspect laboratories and animal facilities at publicly supported institutions. Institutions could lose funding if deficiencies noted by the committees are not corrected.

71. Chambers, K. Tate and Cathleen Hines. "Recent Developments Concerning the Use of Animals in Medical Research." <u>Journal of Legal Medicine</u>, v. 4, March 1983, pp. 109-129.

Explains the controversy between medical researchers and animal rights advocates; provides a history of animal cruelty laws; summarizes relevant federal and state laws; summarizes and critiques several proposed legal solutions to the problem; and presents issues for further consideration.

72. Clarke, Maxine. "Animals in Research: U.S. Rules to Be Made Tighter." <u>Nature</u>, v. 317, September 12, 1985, p. 103.

Describes National Institutes of Health guidelines on laboratory animal welfare and a bill expected to be submitted to Congress which would considerably strengthen those regulations.

73. "Double-Talk on Animals: NIH Seems More Ready to Risk Its Reputation Than to Meet Serious Critics on Animal Care." Nature, v. 309, May 3, 1984, p. 2.
     The National Institutes of Health is trying to counter antivivisectionists' advertising campaigns which feature cute, furry animals by holding meetings around the country featuring human patients and their families who have benefited from animal experiments. NIH has proposed new regulations for the care and use of animals and proposed legislation to limit abuses.

74. Ellis, Gary B. "Necessary Fuss." BioScience, v. 36, June 1986, p. 356.
     This editorial states that scientists, animal welfare advocates, and laboratory animals all benefited from the federal legislation and Public Health Service policy passed in 1985. The new laws and policy mandate reduction in animal use, replacement of animals when possible, and refinement of procedures.

75. "Federal Agencies Agree on Use of Lab Animals." Public Heath Reports, v. 100, September-October 1985, pp. 552-553.
     U.S. government agencies have committed themselves to new government policies, effective June 1, 1985, which address issues such as pain, the selection of appropriate species and numbers of animals used in testing, research, and training.

76. Fox, Jeffrey L. "Changes in Animal Care Policy Proposed." Science, v. 224, April 27, 1984, pp. 364-365.
     The National Institutes of Health, reacting in part to pressure from animal activists, has proposed stricter guidelines for the treatment of experimental animals. Institutional animal research committees including lay persons not affiliated with the research institution would be appointed to review the experimental use of animals. Reactions of scientists and animal welfare proponents are reported.

77. Fox, Jeffrey L. "Lab Animal Welfare Issue Gathers Momentum." Science, v. 223, February 3, 1984, pp. 468-469.
     The views of the extremist and more moderate animal rights groups in the U.S. are recounted and the laboratory animal welfare bills before Congress, federal legislation still to be proposed, and local and state legislative activity are described.

31

78.   Holden, Constance.   "HHS Revises Rules on Animal Research." Science, v. 228, May 17, 1985, p. 830.
        Revisions to Public Health Service policy on animals in labs funded by the PHS require institutional animal use and care committees, stricter specifications for facilities, accreditation or self-assessment based on National Institutes of Health guidelines, and detailed reporting to government. Other initiatives to protect animals are also reported.

79.   Inglehart, John K.   "The Use of Animals in Research." New England Journal of Medicine, v. 13, August 8, 1985, pp. 395-400.
        Discusses existing federal policy as well as proposed legislation that would extend the government's animal use regulations. The new National Institutes of Health policy on care and use of laboratory animals and some particular instances whereby the mishandling of animals has been brought to public and governmental attention by animal welfare advocates are included.

80.   Lewis, P. B.   "Animal Welfare Hearings Conducted." BioScience, v. 33, October 1983, pp. 541-542.
        American Institute of Biological Sciences Executive Director Charles M. Chambers testified in support of a Senate bill which would enact improved standards for laboratory animals. The AIBS encourages institutions to monitor animal use to insure proper care and humane treatment of animals. Opposition groups also testified.

81.   McDonald, Karen L.   "Creating a Private Cause of Action Against Abusive Animal Research." University of Pennsylvania Law Review, v. 134, January 1986, pp. 399-432.
        Animal rights groups should be given power, under state anti-cruelty laws, to stop abuse of animals in laboratories. Federal laws, giving scientists control over research, are inadequate.

82.   Miller, J. A. "Looking Out for Animal Research." Science News, v. 125, April 21, 1984, p. 247.
        In an effort to protect research on animals in the face of legislative efforts by animal welfare groups, the National Institutes of Health proposed changes in the animal use policies followed by its grantees. In some areas, the NIH changes are more extensive than the legislative proposals.

83. Mishkin, Barbara. "On Parallel Tracks: Protecting Human Subjects and Animals." <u>Hastings Center Report</u>, v. 15, October 1985, pp. 36-37.
     Federal grantees must have institutional review boards which review research protocols involving human subjects. National Institutes of Health policies and proposed federal legislation call for similar animal care and use committees. Scientists should participate in the legislative process since similar research controls will surely be enacted.

84. **Moss, Thomas H.** **"The Modern Politics of Laboratory Animal Use."** <u>**Science, Technology and Human Values**</u>**, v. 9, Spring 1984, pp. 51-56. Reprinted in** <u>**BioScience**</u>**, v. 34, November 1984, pp. 621-625.**
     Potential legislative advances are possible as research scientists and animal welfare advocates relinquish their "automatic attitudes" and "reflex" rejections of each other's needs. Scientists' professional organizations have shown such progress by endorsing legislation to strengthen the Animal Welfare Act and the role of institutional animal care committees.

85. "New Animal Welfare Rules." <u>Science News</u>, v. 128, November 2, 1985, p. 28.
     The Public Health Service is requiring that all researchers funded by PHS must either establish that their animal programs are accredited by the American Association for Accreditation of Laboratory Animal Care or submit a detailed report on their animal care programs.

86. "NIH Proposes Change in Animal Care and Use Policies." <u>BioScience</u>, v. 34, July/August 1984, p. 413.
     Proposed changes would specify the membership of institutional animal research committees, clarify the committees' responsibilities, and create a mechanism for institutions to show their compliance with the new policies.

87. Overcast, Thomas D. and Bruce D. Sales. "Regulation of Animal Experimentation." <u>JAMA: Journal of the American Medical Association</u>, v. 254, October 11, 1985, pp. 1944-1949.
     Summarizes the animal experimentation controversy, recounts the history of animal "cruelty" laws, and describes the present state and federal laws regulating the use of animals in research. Proposed legislation sponsored by animal rights advocates is criticized. It would be "foolhardy" for legislators to enact laws against research that would ultimately benefit their constituents.

88. Pavelock, Lisa A. "Towards Legal Rights for Laboratory Animals?" <u>Journal of Legislation</u>, v. 10, Winter 1983, pp. 198-212.
     Proposed legislation to restrict animal use is described. Since animals have been used throughout the history of science and are still used in scientific research and drug and product testing, it is difficult to pass restrictive legislation.

89. Rosner, Fred. **"Is Animal Experimentation Being Threatened by Animal Rights Groups?"** <u>**JAMA: Journal of the American Medical Association**</u>**, v. 254, October 11, 1985, pp. 1942-1943.**
     Vocal and violent animal rights activity has led to increased federal and state legislation, the provisions of which are presented. Scientists must continue to explain the importance of their research to the public and to perfect the mechanisms that insure humane care and ethical use of animals in their laboratories.

90. Stevens, Christine. "Mistreatment of Laboratory Animals Endangers Biomedical Research." <u>Nature</u>, v. 311, September 27, 1984, pp. 295-297.
     Passage of proposed federal legislation would correct deficiencies in the Animal Welfare Act by preventing needless suffering. Examples of improper animal care in academic experimental laboratories are presented.

91. Sun, Marjorie. "Animal Welfare and Fetal Research in Bill on NIH." <u>Science</u>, v. 220, April 22, 1983, p. 389.

     A proposed amendment on animal welfare requires annual inspections of scientists' laboratories and institutional animal welfare committees which include a veterinarian and a person not affiliated with that institution. Other bills are also described.

92. Sun, Marjorie. "A Push for Animal Welfare Bills." <u>Science</u>, v. 221, August 12, 1983, p. 633.

     Proposed federal and California legislation would regulate the treatment of animals, require evaluation of current animal use, and provide funds for studying alternative experimental techniques. The use of pound animals and the military's study of gunshot wounds in animals is also discussed.

93. U.S. Congress. House of Representatives. Committee on Agriculture. Subcommittee on Department Operations, Research, and Foreign Agriculture. <u>Improved Standards for Laboratory Animals Act and Enforcement of the Animal Welfare Act by the Animal and Plant Health Inspection Service</u>. Washington, DC: Government Printing Office, 1985. Superintendent of Documents number Y4.Ag8/1:98-86.

     Hearings on a bill which mandates institutional animal care committees, use of painkilling drugs for research animals, and a national database of experiments to help eliminate unnecessary duplication of research effort.

94. U.S. Congress. House of Representatives. Committee on Energy and Commerce. Subcommittee on Health and the Environment. <u>Humane Care for Animals in Research</u>. Washington, DC: Government Printing Office, 1983. Superintendent of Documents number Y4.En2/3:97-189.

     Hearings on a bill to improve conditions under which animals are used and encourage research into methods which would enable a reduction in the use of animals.

95. U.S. Congress. House of Representatives. Committee on Science and Technology. Subcommittee on Science, Research and Technology. Humane Care and Development of Substitutes for Animals in Research Act. Washington, DC: Government Printing Office, 1983. Superintendent of Documents number Y4.Sci2:97/147.

   Hearings on a bill which requires the development of alternative techniques to reduce animal use and pain, accreditation of laboratories, lay person and veterinarian representation on institutional animal care committees, and scientific peer review panels.

96. U.S. Congress. Senate. Committee on Agriculture, Nutrition, and Forestry. Improved Standards for Laboratory Animals. Washington, DC: Government Printing Office, 1984. Superintendent of Documents number Y4.Ag8/3:S.hrg.98-470.

   Hearings on a bill requiring institutional animal care committees including at least one member not affiliated with the institution to assure humane practices and use of alternatives and relevant information and to inspect laboratories and report to the Department of Agriculture.

97. U.S. Department of Health and Human Services. National Institutes of Health. Guide for the Care and Use of Laboratory Animals. rev. ed. Bethesda, MD: National Institutes of Health, 1985. (NIH Publication no. 85-23).

   This guide provides requirements and recommendations which are to be followed by scientists who use animals in their research.

98. U.S. National Institutes of Health. Office for Protection from Research Risks. Public Health Service Policy on Humane Care and Use of Laboratory Animals, revised as of September 1986. Bethesda, MD: National Institutes of Health, 1986. Superintendent of Documents number HE20.3002:L11/13.

   Incorporates changes in Public Health Service policy mandated by the Health Research Extension Act of 1985. More institutions are covered by the policy, requirements for animal care and use committees are specified, institutions must describe training programs in humane animal use, and must train personnel in the concept, use, and availability of alternative techniques.

99.   Weiss, Laura B.   "Scientists Oppose Legislation: Congress Urged to Require Better Treatment of Animals Used in Scientific Research."   <u>Congressional Quarterly Weekly Report</u>, v. 40, November 13, 1982, pp. 2855-2857.
     Bills introduced into the Senate and House of Representatives would require animal care committees, standards for animal care and treatment, funding to develop alternatives to the use of animals, and accreditation of laboratories.   The history of U.S. animal welfare legislation and the views of researchers and animal welfare advocates are described.

100.   Wortman, Judith.   "AIBS Joins to Increase Animal Welfare Funds."   <u>BioScience</u>, v. 34, June 1984, p. 357.
     The American Institute of Biological Sciences recommends a centralized, well trained group of federal officials to ensure adequate inspections and adherence to scientific research standards.   Additional funding is proposed.

101.   Wortman, Judith.   "PHS Revises Its Lab Animal Welfare Policy."   <u>BioScience</u>, v. 35, July/August 1985, p. 408.
     New Public Health Service policy requires institutions funded by PHS to: comply with new National Institutes of Health guidelines for animal care and use, describe their accreditation or perform a self-evaluation, describe the qualifications and responsibilities of their program veterinarian, describe the membership and procedures for the institutional care committee, describe a heath program for workers, and provide a species inventory for each facility.

U.S. State Legislation Concerning Animal Experimentation

102. Fox, Jeffrey L. "Animal Rights Bill Defeated in California." Science, v. 224, June 29, 1984, p. 1414.
    A California bill to restrict all research on pound animals was defeated and a Maryland bill was clarified to specify steps to be taken before research animals are confiscated by authorities. Scientists influenced outcomes in both states.

103. Fox, Jeffrey L. "Massachusetts Forbids Use of Impounded Pets in Labs." Science, v. 223, January 13, 1984, p. 151.
    Massachusetts has the broadest and most stringent controls of any U.S. state on the use of animals in research. Biomedical scientists supported the law, which prevents them from obtaining research animals from pounds, in order to head off more restrictive legislation.

104. Herbert, W. "State Law Halts Pet Research Projects." Science News, v. 125, January 14, 1984, p. 21.
    Massachusetts legislation, supported by both researchers and "anti-vivisectionists," prohibits the sale of stray dogs and cats to medical research laboratories. Breeding kennels will supply research animals, but at a greater monetary cost than that paid for pound animals.

105. Sun, Marjorie. "California Universities Block Animal Rights Bill." Science, v. 221, September 2, 1983, p. 934.
    Stanford University and the University of California successfully lobbied to withdraw proposed legislation which would have prohibited the importation of pound animals for experimental use.

The International Scene

106. "Animals Also Have Rights." <u>New Statesman</u>, v. 108, November 23, 1984, p. 3.

This editorial makes the point that relatively few experiments actually benefit humans. New British legislation should demand that products to be tested uniquely meet a genuine human need and no alternative testing methods are available.

107. "Animals White Paper Pleases Nobody." <u>New Scientist</u>, v. 106, May 23, 1985, p. 5.

A supplemental position paper on animal experimentation, released by the British government, is not acceptable to the scientists' Research Defense Society nor to the antivivisectionists' Mobilisation of Laboratory Rights organization. Details of the objections are reported.

108. Beardsley, Tim. "Canada Baboon Cruelty Trial." <u>Nature</u>, v. 313, February 7, 1985, p. 421.

A Canadian physiologist and the chief veterinarian at the University of Western Ontario have both been charged under the Canadian criminal code for causing unnecessary pain, suffering or injury to an animal. The complaint was filed by the group "Lifeforce" as a result of the researcher's experiments on lipid metabolism in the baboon.

109. Beardsley, Tim. "UK Animal Welfare: Government Plans Upset RSPCA." <u>Nature</u>, v. 305, October 20, 1983, p. 662.

The Royal Society for the Prevention of Cruelty to Animals asserts that British legislation proposed to control animal pain and suffering is inadequate. The Home Secretary should be responsible for and answerable to Parliament on issues involving animal experiments.

110. Britt, David. "Animal Experiments." <u>New Scientist</u>, v. 104, October 4, 1984, p. 2.

A proponent of animal care committees recounts the arguments rendered by scientists and animal welfare advocates concerning these committees which would review the ethics of proposed animal experiments in British laboratories.

111. Britt, David. "Ethics, Ethical Committees and Animal Experimentation." <u>Nature</u>, v. 311, October 11, 1984, pp. 503-506.
    A proponent of the introduction of ethical review committees in Britain describes the history and function of such committees in Sweden, the United States, and Canada. These committees check experiments for potential animal suffering and could conceivably judge scientific merit as well.

112. Cherfas, Jeremy. "Lab Animals Could Suffer Under Euro-Law." <u>New Scientist</u>, v. 93, February 25, 1982, p. 485.
    The British Home Office disagees with Europe's draft convention on animal welfare because the convention would provide exemptions to the "pain clause" which, under present British law, forbids inflicting severe and enduring pain on animals.

113. Clarke, Maxine. "UK Laboratory Animals: Debate on Legislation Ahead." <u>Nature</u>, v. 318, November 21, 1985, p. 201.
    A new British bill which would reform existing legislation on laboratory animals is supported by scientists and by "middle-of-the-road" animal welfare groups but is opposed by extremist groups who are against all animal experimentation.

114. Clarke, Maxine. "UK Laboratory Animals: Experimentation Reduced." <u>Nature</u>, v. 316, July 25, 1985, p. 286.
    The number of British experiments on living animals decreased 4% over the previous year, a sign that researchers are reacting to pressure from public opinion. Details of current and proposed legislation in Britain are summarized.

115. Clarke, Maxine. "UK Laboratory Animals: New Legislation Forecast." <u>Nature</u>, v. 315, May 23, 1985, p. 267.
    The British government's second "White Paper" on Scientific Procedures on Living Animals specifies tighter controls on the severity of experimental procedures, stricter procedures to obtain a license to experiment, improvements in the care of animals, and higher penalties for offenses.

116. Dickson, David. "Swiss Voters Reject Ban on Vivisection." <u>Science</u>, v. 230, December 13, 1985, p. 1257.

Swiss voters rejected a proposed constitutional amendment which would have forbidden vivisection of vertebrate animals and all cruel experiments on animals. Antivivisectionists plan to propose a less severe amendment calling for a reduction in experiments on animals.

117. Hollands, Clive. <u>Compassion is the Bugler: The Struggle for Animal Rights</u>. Edinburgh: Macdonald Publishers, 1980. 201p.

Documents the history of recent efforts in the United Kingdom to involve a coalition of animal welfare groups in the political process in order to persuade the political parties to declare their intentions regarding animal experimentation and farming methods.

118. "Law of the Union of Soviet Socialist Republics on the Protection and Utilization of the Animal World." <u>Current Digest of the Soviet Press</u>, v. 32, August 20, 1980, pp. 10-14+.

Translated into English, this text of Soviet law refers to the use of animals for hunting, fishing, scientific, educational, and industrial purposes. The law allows for restrictions on the use of animals and provides for the protection of animals, record keeping, and state supervision.

119. Lubinska, Anna. "Brussels May Step in to Control Experiments." <u>New Scientist</u>, v. 96, December 16, 1982, p. 708.

The European Economic Community, under a revised Treaty of Rome, may be given extended jurisdiction to prevent abusive exploitation of animals for purposes of laboratory experimentation and trade in wild animals.

120. MacKenzie, Debora. "German Scientists Rail at Animal Welfare Law." <u>New Scientist</u>, v. 110, May 1, 1986, p. 20.

German scientists say that they will move their experiments out of the country if a new law requiring them to ask permission to perform animal experiments is passed. Committees, including members of animal welfare groups, would have to approve the experiments.

121.   MacKenzie, Debora.   "Swiss to Vote on Ban on Vivisection." New Scientist, v. 108, November 28, 1985, p. 17.
     On December 1, 1985, the Swiss will vote on a referendum to decide whether to severely limit experiments on animals by making researchers who harm animals liable to the same penalties as those for harming humans.   Arguments for and against the proposal are presented.

122.   McKay, Shona.   "A Sacrifice in the Name of Research." Macleans, v. 95, June 28, 1982, pp. 50-51.
     Although Canada has no federal legislation to protect laboratory animals, public and professional awareness is growing.   A report on animal research in public institutions documents 62 experiments.   Amid public outcry against certain experiments, the Canadian Council on Animal Care is scrutinizing particular experiments and federal monies are being used to train scientists in alternative research methods.

123.   Neffe, Jurgen.   "Animal Protection: Critics Assail West German Law." Nature, v. 321, May 1, 1986, p. 5.
     Scientists oppose the new West German law which requires research projects to be approved by commissions, one third of whose membership may be animal welfare advocates.   Animals may not be used to develop and test weapons, tobacco products, cleaning products, and cosmetics.   Alternative techniques are encouraged.

124.   "Protection for Laboratory Animals?" Nature, v. 293, September 17, 1981, pp. 173-174.
     This editorial recounts aspects of the British Cruelty to Animals Act of 1876, reasons that legislative change is necessary, and tells why the scientific community cannot ignore arguments against laboratory experiments on animals.   Institutional committees, empowered to approve or withhold approval of proposed experiments, are advocated.   Letters of reaction to this editorial are published on page 506.

125.   Swinbanks, David.   "Animal Welfare: Laboratory Animals Unprotected." Nature, v. 322, July 10, 1986, p. 103.

A French researcher has taken her findings about Japanese mistreatment of experimental monkeys to the French press after being unable to effect change from her research position at Japan's key primate research center. Animal welfare at the center has since improved although there are still no Japanese government requirements for review, reporting, or licensing of experiments.

126.   Vines, Gail.   "How Germany Vetoed New Laws on Animal Pain." New Scientist, v. 96, December 16, 1982, p. 708.

The final draft of a European "convention" to protect animals was revised to suit the West Germans, whose constitution guarantees freedom of scientific research. Major pharmaceutical countries of Europe also lobbied for the changes which would continue to allow painful experimentation.

127.   Wenz, Charles.   "Laboratory Animals: European Convention in Sight?" Nature, v. 302, March 24, 1983, p. 284.

A committee of the 21 nation Council of Europe nears the end of its deliberations to draft a "convention for the protection of animals used for experimental purposes." British committee members are being pressured by animal welfare groups who want a total ban on the use of animals in research as well as by the more moderate Royal Society for the Prevention of Cruelty to Animals.

128.   Wenz, Charles.   "Laboratory Animals: Replacement for 1876 Act in Sight." Nature, v. 303, May 19, 1983, p. 191.

The British government published a "White Paper" specifying its proposals for legislation on animal experimentation.   Differences between existing legislation, dated 1876, and these new proposals are described.

43

Laboratory Tests, Experiments, and Conditions

129.   Fox, Michael W.   <u>Laboratory Animal Husbandry:</u> <u>Ethology, Welfare and Experimental Variables</u>.   Albany: State University of New York Press, 1986. 267p.
     In order to do good research leading to good medical applications, the scientist must tend to the behavioral, social, and psychological, as well as the physical needs of animal subjects. Discusses variables such as social deprivation, handling, genetics, lighting, noise, and food, as well as the broader issues of animal rights and humane attitudes in the quest for more holistic biomedical research and practice.

130.   Greenberg, Gary and Charles Burdsal.   "Animal Colony Practices in North American Academic Institutions: A Survey." <u>The Journal of General Psychology</u>, v. 106, April 1982, pp. 165-173.
     Wide variation exists in the physical conditions and animal management practices in psychology departments in United States and Canadian academic institutions. Experiments, particularly those involving replication, could suffer from inadequate control of outside influences.

131. Heneson, Nancy. "American Agencies Denounce LD50 Test." <u>New Scientist</u>, v. 100, November 17, 1983, p. 475.
     At a meeting on acute toxicity testing, representatives of various U.S. government agencies endorsed a modified version of the LD50 test which uses fewer animals. Industry, however, will not abandon the original LD50 until government gives a "clear signal" that the new test is acceptable.

132.   James, Carollyn.   "A Rabbit's-Eye View." <u>Science'84</u>, v. 5, March 1984, pp. 88-89.
     In the Draize test, liquids such as shampoos are dropped into rabbits' eyes to test for sensitivity. Pros and cons of the Draize test and new, alternative testing methods are discussed.

133. Leccese, Michael. "Of Mice and Monkeys: Animal Research in Space Is Once Again a Hot Issue." Space World, v. 8-260, August 1985, pp. 16-18.

Animal activists argue that animals should be eliminated from space research because they cannot volunteer and that the experiments are irrelevant because there are no animals in space. NASA maintains that the experiments are crucial in order to determine the effects of space travel on humans.

134. Mayo, Deborah G. "Against a Scientific Justification of Animal Experiments." In Miller, Harlan B. and William H. Williams. Ethics and Animals. Clifton, NJ: Humana Press, 1983. pp. 339-359. (Contemporary Issues in Biomedicine, Ethics, and Society.)

Counters the argument that painful and lethal experimentation is necessary in order to provide basic scientific knowledge and the health, safety, and comfort of humans and demonstrates, by citing actual studies, that much animal experimentation is not scientifically valid or relevant. Laboratory conditions do not accurately reflect nature, species differ, variables are not always adequately controlled, and the questions asked are often trivial, obvious, or already answered.

135. "NIH Starts Program in Animal-Use Education." Chemical & Engineering News, v. 62, April 16, 1984, p. 10.

The National Institutes of Health has begun a program to educate scientists and the public on animal welfare and the proper use of animals in health research. NIH held a symposium and plans regional workshops, a guidebook for researchers, an inventory of audio-visual materials, and distribution of printed materials to the public.

136. Pratt, Dallas. Painful Experiments on Animals. New York: Argus Archives, 1976. 207p.

The bulk of this book recounts specific experiments on animals carried out in the 1970's in New York and New Jersey. Toxicological testing, pain and stress testing, and surgical and radiation experiments are included. Then current United States and New York regulations for laboratory animal care are described.

137. Rall, David P. and George Roush, Jr. "Is Animal Testing Overrated? Two Views." EPA Journal, v. 10, December 1984, pp. 16-19.
     Animal studies will remain the primary means to determine toxicity, carcinogenicity, mechanisms of drug action and effective doses of potentially toxic chemotherapeutic substances. We must use caution in accepting the results of single species studies and should use multiple species, biochemical, pharmacokinetic, and epidemiological studies as well.

138. Ryder, Richard. "Experiments on Animals." In Regan, Tom and Peter Singer. Animal Rights and Human Obligations. Englewood Ciffs, NJ: Prenctice-Hall, 1976. pp. 33-47.
     This chapter is identical to the first part of Ryder's essay (no. 139).

139. Ryder, Richard. "Experiments on Animals." In Godlovitch, Stanley, Roslind Godlovitch, and John Harris. Animals, Men and Morals: An Enquiry into the Maltreatment of Non-Humans. New York: Taplinger, 1972. pp. 41-82.
     Statistics, descriptions of types of experiments, and excerpts from scientific journals reveal the procedures used on animals in experimental laboratories. Reviews existing British law and proposed amendments and argues for the basic rights of animals based upon scientists' claims of the similarities between humans and other animals.

140. Sun, Marjorie. "Lots of Talk About LD50." Science, v. 222, December 9, 1983, p. 1106.
     While scientists and animal rights groups agree that the LD50 test is outdated, of limited value, and use of the test is declining, researchers continue to use it in the belief that it is required by federal regulatory agencies. Food and Drug Administration officials state that the test is not required. Other agencies require a modified version that uses fewer animals.

141. Widdowson, Elsie M. "Animals in the Service of Human Nutrition." Nutrition Today, v. 20, September/October 1985, pp. 33-40.
     Recounts the history of the use of experimental animals as applied to human nutrition and discusses the applicability to humans of results obtained on animals, current difficulties in using animals, and the increased use of humans in nutrition experimentation.

142. Wills, Carol.   "Beauty and the Beasts."   New Statesman, v. 109, May 10, 1985, p. 10.
     In response to strong criticism of the testing of cosmetics on animals, several British cosmetics firms have adopted policies of not using animals in testing. Tests such as the Draize eye and patch tests are described.

Primate Experimentation

143. Beardsley, Tim. "Monkey Business: Bolivia Asks for Animals Back." <u>Nature</u>, v. 319, February 20, 1986, p. 610.

Three hundred sixty-one owl and squirrel monkeys, considered endangered species, were exported from Bolivia to the United States under an exemption to Bolivia's law prohibiting animal export. The Bolivian government demanded the return of the monkeys, destined for use in malaria vaccine research, after the Bolivian press reported that they were to be sold as pets.

144. Fox, Jeffrey L. "Chimps in Research." <u>BioScience</u>, v. 35, February 1985, pp. 75-76.

Chimpanzees, considered essential by scientists for the study of diseases such as AIDS and hepatitis, are becoming scarce due to protective agreements and the difficulty of breeding in captivity. A controversial draft National Chimpanzee Management Plan calls for establishing a breeding colony, temporarily decreasing chimp use by researchers, and killing older animals who are unable to breed or who have been exposed to a specific form of hepatitis.

145. **King, Frederick A. and Cathy J. Yarbrough. "Medical and Behavioral Benefits from Primate Research."** <u>**The Physiologist**</u>, v. 28, April 1985, pp. 75-87.

A literature review recounting many of the contributions of research on primates, which are very similar behaviorally and biologically to humans, to human health and welfare.

146. Linden, Eugene. "Endangered Chimps in the Lab." <u>New York Times Magazine</u>, v. 132, December 19, 1982, pp. 77-88.

Describes the use of chimpanzees, endangered species in the wild, for medical and psychological research. Some of the chimps used in this research are the ones previously taught sign language in communication experiments. Ethical and philosophical issues are raised.

147. Sun, Marjorie. "Primate Centers Brace for Protests." <u>Science</u>, v. 219, March 4, 1983, p. 1049.
Animal welfare activist groups plan major demonstrations at federally funded primate research centers. The groups claim that many good alternatives exist which could replace animal experimentation. They also demand the closing of some of the primate centers.

148. Torrey, Lee. "The Agony of Primate Research." <u>Science Digest</u> v. 92, May 1984, pp. 70-72.
Specific experiments on monkeys are described. A case is made for lessened experimentation on primates and better care when they must be used, since they are frequently subject to injury and death when caught, shipped, housed, and handled.

Animal Experimentation in the Classroom

149. Cliburn, Joseph W. "Dear Editor." <u>The American Biology Teacher</u>, v. 48, March 1986, p. 137.

This response to Santopoalo (no. 159) claims that dissection is integral to the study of anatomy and animal experimentation is integral to the study of physiology. Better teaching is called for rather than the elimination of dissection.

150. Henig, Robin Marantz. "Animal Welfare Groups Press for Limits on High School Research." <u>BioScience</u>, v. 29, November 1979, pp. 651-653.

At a conference on the use of animals in high school classes, it was charged that teachers and students are often not adequately trained to care for animals or to learn much from them. Science fair experiments in particular drew strong criticism and Science Fair Rules (1980) are excerpted. Alternatives to painful experiments were suggested.

151. Holden, Constance. "NASA Student Rat Project Questioned." <u>Science</u>, v. 217, July 30, 1982, p. 425.

NASA is concerned over potential reaction in the animal welfare community from allowing a student project involving arthritic rats to fly in the space shuttle.

152. Igelsrud, Don. "Dear Editor." <u>The American Biology Teacher</u>, v. 48, March 1986, pp. 136-137.

A response to Santopoalo (no. 159) maintaining that dissection of animals, conducted without causing pain or discomfort, is important in biology education. When teachers teach about animals' reactions, students become more sensitive to animals rather than insensitive.

153. **Mayer, William V. et al. <u>Perspectives on the Educational Use of Animals</u>. New York: The Myrin Institute, 1980. 77p. (Proceedings, Number 36, The Myrin Institute.)**

Students can learn a lot of biology, as well as develop appreciation and concern for nonhuman life, by observing animals living in the classroom or field. Experiments which cause harm to animals should not be done at the school level and alternatives are suggested.

154. McGiffin, Heather and Nancie Brownley, eds. <u>Animals in Education: Use of Animals in High School Biology Classes and Science Fairs</u>. Washington, DC: The Institute for the Study of Animal Problems, 1980. 160p.

Biology students' study of animals is necessary, but experiments which cause animal suffering or stress cannot be justified. Educational objectives, use of vertebrates, science fairs, state laws, and animal rights are discussed. Humane and noninvasive studies of animal behavior, structure and function in the wild, zoos and lab are recommended.

155. "NABT Guidelines for the Use of Live Animals." <u>The American Biology Teacher</u>, v. 48, February 1986, pp. 121-122.

On April 27, 1985, the National Association of Biology Teachers adopted new guidelines which call for humane and respectful treatment of animals under direct supervision by competent science teachers and biomedical scientists. The text of the guidelines is presented.

156. "NABT Guidelines for the Use of Live Animals at the Pre-University Level." <u>The American Biology Teacher</u>, v. 42, October 1980, pp. 426-427.

The National Association of Biology Teachers guidelines call for humane treatment and care of animals under direct supervision by appropriately trained faculty. Use of "lower" orders of life are preferred when possible and the use of agents known to cause deleterious effects are not allowed.

157. Palca, Joseph. "Guidelines Off." <u>Nature</u>, v. 319, February 6, 1986, p. 440.

The National Academy of Sciences will not endorse the new, less restrictive, guidelines for the use of animals in U.S. elementary and secondary schools proposed by the National Science Teachers Association. Older guidelines prohibit surgery and experimental procedures which cause pain, while newer rules prohibit "unnecessary" pain and permit supervised surgery.

158. Rowan, Andrew N. "Animals in Education." <u>The American Biology Teacher</u>, v. 43, May 1981, pp. 280-282.

Conference members studying the use of vertebrates in secondary schools and science fairs reached the consensus that the study of live animals is essential in biology education. There was strong disagreement, however, on the extracurricular and science fair use of animals, particularly concerning levels of skill and supervision of students.

159. Santopoalo, Tina. "Stop Condoning Cruelty to Animals." <u>The American Biology Teacher</u>, v. 47, November/December 1985, p. 454.

In a letter to the editor, Santopoalo maintains that classroom dissection of animals is crude and unnecessary and desensitizes students. She also objects to repetitive experiments which inflict suffering on animals and suggests alternative approaches to the teaching of biology and psychology.

160. Sieber, Joan E. "Students' and Scientists' Attitudes on Animal Research." <u>The American Biology Teacher</u>, v. 48, February 1986, pp. 85-91.

Scientists who were interviewed about their experiences with animal experimentation in the classroom felt that they had reconciled their "tender" feelings towards animals with the necessity to use them in research and that discussion of ethics and humane treatment was appropriate only for advanced or graduate students. The students, however, had not satisfactorily resolved the dilemma, felt they did not receive appropriate help from their teachers, and wanted opportunities to study humane treatment and ethical problems.

161. Sun, Marjorie. "Science Teachers To Ban Testing Harmful to Animals." <u>Science</u>, v. 209, August 15, 1980, p. 791.

The National Association of Biology Teachers and the National Science Teachers Association have adopted guidelines banning classroom experiments which harm animals. Animal welfare groups are still concerned with extracurricular projects such as those performed for science fairs.

Animal Welfare Activists and Their Activities

162. "Animal Researchers Spurn Gutter Press." New Scientist, v. 87, September 4, 1980, p. 694.

Animal liberationists who broke into England's Institute of Animal Physiology accused researchers of animal cruelty and torture. The scientists defended their research and the policy of barring journalists from visiting the Institute.

163. Barnes, Deborah M. "Tight Money Squeezes Out Animal Models." Science, v. 232, April 18, 1986. pp. 309-311.

Funding cutbacks, some due to pressure from animal rights groups, are causing researchers to eliminate animal colonies which provide models for the study of human diseases and normal body functions. The National Research Council has established a new committee to study the situation and issue an assessment.

164. Blakeslee, Sandra. "Animal Rights: Battle Joined on Animal Lib." Nature, v. 315, June 20, 1985, p. 625.

Researchers want the California legislature to impose stiff penalties on "animal liberators" who disrupt research by releasing laboratory animals and vandalizing scientific facilities. Specific animal lib activities in California are described.

165. Holden, Constance. "Centers Targeted by Activists." Science, v. 232, April 11, 1986, p. 149.

This roundup lists research centers which have been raided by animal liberation activists and describes their actions as well as the reactions of federal agencies and the targeted institutions.

166. Lauer, Margaret. "Animal Rights Commandos." Mother Jones, v. 8, September-October 1983, p. 9.

Scientists are beginning to "clean up their acts" in reaction to raids by militant animal activists who break into labs to steal animals and wreck offices and files. Cruel sounding experiments and a break-in at Howard University are described.

167. Lauer, Margaret. "A Champion of Animal Rights."
<u>Progressive</u>, v. 48, April 1984, pp. 14-15.
     Activist Henry Spira worked to cause drug companies
to reduce their use of the Draize irritancy test and fund
research on alternatives to animal testing. He also
helped induce the Food and Drug Administration to
eliminate the requirement that drug companies utilize the
LD50 toxicity test.

168. Nevin, David. "Scientist Helps Stir New Movement
for 'Animal Rights.'" <u>Smithsonian</u>, v. 11, April 1980,
pp. 50-59.
     The concerns and activities of Michael W. Fox, a
veterinarian, animal rights "crusader", and former
experimenter, are described. Conditions in laboratories
and on farms are reported and alternatives suggested.

169. Quinn, Hal. "Fighting to Free Animals." <u>Macleans</u>,
v. 97, December 3, 1984, p. 58.
     Activist animal welfare groups in England took
responsibility for over 250 operations including claiming
to have poisoned candy produced by a company which funds
animal research. They freed animals involved in
experiments at a college and broke into scientists'
homes. In Toronto, a hunger strike by activists ended
with researchers refusing to halt experiments.

170. Weiner, Jonathan. "Animal Liberation."
<u>Cosmopolitan</u>, v. 188, June 1980, pp. 142-150+.
     Describes the animal rights philosophy and recounts
the work of activists who "liberate" animals from
scientific laboratories and actively demonstrate to stop
animal experiments.

Reports of Specific Animal Experimentation Cases

171. "Animal-Abuse Case Update." Science News, v. 128, October 12, 1985, p. 230.

The National Institutes of Health continued its suspension of funding for the University of Pennsylvania head injury research involving baboons. Funding could be restored pending certain changes and written assurance of compliance with NIH guidelines for the care and use of nonhuman primates. The project would undergo five years of probationary scrutiny.

172. "Animal Cruelty Charged in Growth Gene Work." Chemical & Engineering News, v. 62, October 8, 1984, p. 5.

The Foundation on Economic Trends, headed by activist Jeremy Rifkin, and the Humane Society of the United States are suing the Department of Agriculture to stop experiments in which a chemical replica of human growth hormone is transferred into pigs and sheep.

173. Beardsley, Tim. "Animal Welfare: Tip-Off Leads to NIH Ban." Nature, v. 318, February 13, 1986, p. 524.

The National Institutes of Health has been making unannounced visits to NIH funded laboratories and suspending the funds of those found in violation of its animal welfare regulations. Columbia University's Health Sciences Division, the City of Hope Medical Center, and the University of Pennsylvania all have had funding suspended.

174. Clarke, Maxine. "Primate Research: NIH Withdraws Support." Nature, v. 317, October 3, 1985, p. 375.

The University of Pennsylvania has banned primate research and reprimanded two of its scientists after disclosure by an animal welfare organization that the guidelines for proper care of animals were not followed. The National Institutes of Health has withdrawn funding and the Department of Agriculture is suing the laboratory for violating the Animal Welfare Act.

175. Cross, Michael. "Rifkin Challenges DNA Implants in Animals." New Scientist, v. 107, July 25, 1985, p. 21.
Activist Jeremy Rifkin is suing the Department of Agriculture, maintaining that recombinant DNA research on farm animals violates provisions of the National Environmental Protection Act by violating the animals' internal environments.

176. Culliton, Barbara. "HHS Halts Animal Experiment." Science, v. 229, August 2, 1985, pp. 447-448.
The National Institutes of Health suspended its funding of University of Pennsylvania researchers who used baboons in their studies of head injuries. Allegations of mistreatment were made by animal rights activists who broke into the laboratories to gather evidence and destroy materials.

177. "Defense Research on Dogs, Cats Stirs Dispute." Chemical & Engineering News, v. 62, October 8, 1984, p. 6.
The Department of Defense first banned all dog and cat experiments and then suspended the ban pending review. Current policies exclude cats and dogs from research on wounds and chemical, biological, and nuclear weapons toxicity.

178. Dorr, Sandra. "Cruelty to Monkeys." Omni, v. 4, March 1982, p. 36.
The case in which Maryland psychologist Edward Taub was convicted of animal cruelty for failing to provide veterinary care to six monkeys is described. His appeal had not yet been heard.

179. Dusheck, J. "Protesters Prompt Halt in Animal Research." Science News, v. 128, July 27, 1985, p. 53.
The National Institutes of Health suspended funds for head injury research on baboons at the University of Pennsylvania. An independent investigation, prompted by Animal Liberation Front activity, showed failure to comply with NIH animal use policy. Animal activists' claims of abuse, scientific fraud and violation of federal guidelines are juxtaposed with scientists' statements of scientific advancement and good research quality.

180. Edwards, Rob. "Video of Animal Pain Shatters Researcher." New Statesman, v. 108, November 23, 1984, p. 6.

   After viewing a videotape provided by animal rights activists, the Scottish neuropathologist who performs post-mortem examinations on baboon brains sent by researchers at the University of Pennsylvania Head Injury Laboratory said he would demand assurances that treatment of the baboons be improved before he would participate further in the studies.

181. Fox, Jeffrey L. "Ban on Shooting Animals for Research is Lifted." Science, v. 223, February 10, 1984, p. 568.

   A military program to study gunshot wounds in live animals was reinstated after it was temporarily halted amid protests that dogs might be targets. Animals such as goats and pigs may be used although Congress has disallowed the use of dogs or cats.

182. Fox, Jeffrey L. "Lab Break-In Stirs Animal Welfare Debate." Science, v. 224, June 22, 1984, pp. 1319-1320.

   Provides descriptions of the head injury research on baboons and the May 1984 break-in and vandalism of the laboratories at the University of Pennsylvania by Animal Liberation Front representatives. Viewpoints of both the research scientists and the animal rights activists are described.

183. Fox, Jeffrey L. "Rifkin Takes Aim at USDA Animal Research." Science, v. 226, October 19, 1984, p. 321.

   Jeremy Rifkin, a social activist, and Michael Fox, a veterinarian representing the Humane Society of America, have filed suit against the Department of Agriculture to block experiments in which genes of one species are transferred into another species. They object to the experiments on environmental, economic, and ethical grounds.

184. Fox, Jeffrey L. "USDA Animal Research Under Fire." BioScience, v. 35, January 1985, pp. 6-7.

   Activists Jeremy Rifkin and Michael Fox have sued to stop biotechnology experiments at the Department of Agriculture where growth hormone genes are being moved between species in order to grow bigger farm animals. Rifkin and Fox object on environmental, economic, and ethical grounds.

185. Heneson, Nancy. "Cruelty to Animals: The State Versus the Scientist." New Scientist, v. 92, December 3, 1981, pp. 672-674.

Heneson describes the case whereby Dr. Edward Taub, a Maryland psychologist who worked with monkeys, had his monkeys seized by the police, his National Institutes of Health grant suspended, and was charged with seventeen counts of animal cruelty. As of November 23, 1981, Taub was found guilty on six counts, not guilty on eleven, and his monkeys were to be returned to him. He was to appeal the verdict.

186. Herbert, W. "Animal Cruelty Verdict Reversed." Science News, v. 124, August 20, 1983, p. 118.

Reports on the reversal of the conviction of Edward Taub by the Maryland Court of Appeals. He had been charged with animal cruelty as a result of his experiments on monkeys. The new ruling was based on the fact that the state anti-cruelty law doesn't apply to federally funded research. Taub had lost his lab and his funding.

187. Herbert, W. "Verdict: Researchers 16, Anti-Vivisectionists 1." Science News, v. 122, July 17, 1982, p. 37.

Describes the case of Edward Taub who was cleared, on appeal, of sixteen of seventeen charges of cruelty to laboratory animals. The NIH suspended Taub's research funding on the grounds that his laboratory did not comply with minimum standards of animal care.

188. Holden, Constance. "Monkey Researcher's Cruelty Verdict Reversed." Science, v. 221, August 26, 1983, p. 839.

Edward Taub's 1981 conviction for neglect of his research monkeys was overturned by the Maryland state appeals court. Taub lost his NIH grant but has a Guggenheim Foundation grant with which he is writing the reports of his research.

189. Holden, Constance. "Police Seize Primates at NIH-Funded Lab." Science, v. 214, October 2, 1981, pp. 32-33.

The police seizure of monkeys from an NIH funded laboratory run by Edward Taub is reported. Taub maintains that the charges of abuse to the animals are "distortions." The NIH is investigating the case.

190. Holden, Constance. "Researcher Charged with Cruelty to Monkeys." Science, v. 214, October 9, 1981, p. 165.
    Edward Taub, the scientist whose research monkeys were seized, has been charged with violation of Maryland's Animal Cruelty Law. The court had ordered the monkeys returned to Taub and they were subsequently kidnapped and finally returned after negotiations with unnamed persons.

191. Holden, Constance. "Scientist Convicted for Monkey Neglect." Science, v. 214, December 11, 1981, pp. 1218-1220.
    A review of the Edward Taub case from the time Alex Pacheco, animal welfare activist, began his work in Taub's lab, up until Taub's conviction on animal cruelty. It does not cover his subsequent successful appeal.

192. "In the Doghouse: Protest Halts Animal Killings." Time, v. 122, August 8, 1983, p. 38.
    A laboratory in which animals would be shot so that military doctors could learn to treat gunshot wounds was prevented from opening after public protests brought the issue to the attention of the Secretary of Defense. Military use of research animals, including such use in four other wound labs, was suspended pending review.

193. Kehrer, Daniel. "The Monkey Snatchers." Science Digest, v. 90, April 1982, pp. 12-14+.
    Details the case in which Edward Taub, a scientist at Maryland's Institute for Behavioral Research, was convicted of cruelty to animals and had his NIH grant suspended. Taub's later successful appeal of his conviction is not included.

194. Lauter, David. "Laboratory Experimentation: Dr. Taub's Animal House." National Law Journal, v. 4, July 5, 1982, p. 11.
    Written during the appeal, this article describes Taub's first trial in which he was convicted of cruelty to his laboratory monkeys. Scientists such as Taub feel that unqualified people are judging research and animal rights activists would not allow any research that hurts animals.

195. Miller, J. A. "Suit Filed Against Hormone-Gene Work." <u>Science News</u>, v. 126, October 13, 1984, p. 229.
Activists Jeremy Rifkin and Michael W. Fox have sued to halt U.S. Department of Agriculture experiments in which human growth hormone is injected into pig and sheep embryos in an attempt to increase growth rate and adult size. The plaintiffs claim that the experiments are cruel towards animals because they are robbed of their unique genetic makeup.

196. "NIH Suspends Funding of Researcher Charged with Animal Cruelty." <u>BioScience</u>, v. 31, November 1981, pp. 714-715.
The National Institutes of Health investigated Edward Taub's laboratory and suspended his funding on the grounds that he failed to comply with NIH guidelines for care and use of laboratory animals. Taub had been charged under Maryland law for cruelty to his laboratory monkeys.

197. Noah, Timothy. "Have You Hugged Your Lab Animal Today? Monkey Business." <u>New Republic</u>, v. 186, June 2, 1982, pp. 20-23.
The Taub case is used to exemplify the stance against animal rights philosophies and activities. Taub is a scapegoat for the anti-vivisection movement, which seeks to "prevent scientists from harming animals to help human beings."

198. **Pacheco, Alex with Anna Francione.** "The Silver Spring Monkeys." In Singer, Peter. <u>In Defense of Animals</u>. New York: Basil Blackwell, 1985. pp. 135-147.
A research assistant who infiltrated Taub's lab tells his account of the case in which Dr. Edward Taub was convicted and then cleared of cruelty to monkeys. Vivid descriptions of laboratory conditions and procedures, the raid during which the monkeys were confiscated, their court ordered return to Taub, and the reversal of that order are all discussed.

199. "Pro and Con: Use Animal Organs for Human Transplants?" U.S. News and World Report, v. 97, November 12, 1984, p. 58.

Two experts disagree on the justification of performing procedures such as the transplantation of a baboon heart into a human baby whose own heart was defective. Jack Provonsha, Director of the Center for Christian Ethics at Loma Linda University, feels that such an operation is justified in order to save a human life. Tom Regan, a Professor of Philosophy, feels that the rights of nonhuman animals are violated by such procedures.

200. Raloff, J. "NIH Limits Animal Studies at Columbia." Science News, v. 129, February 8, 1986, p. 85.

Pursuant to accreditation rules effective December 31, 1985, the NIH issued its first suspension of research funds, finding Columbia University's Health Sciences Division deficient in its animal care procedures.

201. Ryan, Tim. "Death of a Seal and the Price of Research." Oceans, v. 19, March/April 1986, pp. 5-6.

A young Hawaiian monk seal, a member of an endangered species, had been used for experimentation because he needed no restraining after having become used to the scientists who cared for him. The experiment, meant to determine how to reduce the high mortality rate in the species, led to muscle damage, lack of eating, kidney damage and, ultimately, death.

202. Sun, Marjorie. "USDA Fines Pennsylvania Animal Laboratory." Science, v. 230, October 25, 1985, p. 423.

Following disclosure of mistreatment of primates in its head injury laboratory, the University of Pennsylvania was fined four thousand dollars by the Department of Agriculture and funding for primate research was suspended by the National Institutes of Health.

Alternatives to Traditional Animal Experimentation

203. "Animals May Escape Eye Tests." New Scientist, v. 99, August 18, 1983, p. 456.

A newly developed toxicity test, to be used on dead animals, could reduce by ninety percent the number of animals used in laboratory experiments.

204. Arehart-Treichel, Joan. "Animal Science From the Animals' Perspective." Science News, v. 122, July 24, 1982, pp. 59-61.

Discusses whether animal experimentation is ethical, describes particular experiments and tests, and recounts measures being taken to lessen the numbers of animals used as well as the pain experienced by those that are still used.

205. Brown, Kitty. "Alternatives to Animal Tests and Other Cruelties." Ms., v. 10, December 1981, p. 45.

Animal tests of toiletry and household products are described along with the funding programs from cosmetics companies and animal welfare agencies which will help develop alternative testing procedures. Nonanimal alternatives have been developed for some cancer research and pregnancy testing.

206. Budiansky, Stephen. "Animal Experimentation: Alternatives Neglected." Nature, v. 315, May 2, 1985, p. 9.

A study supported by the National Institutes of Health suggests that scientists who work on "unconventional" or nonanimal models, have difficulty securing funding for their research.

207. "Detecting Carcinogens." The Economist, v. 282, February 27, 1982, pp. 86-87.

Chemicals should first be tested for carcinogenicity using nonanimal methods since animal tests use many animals, are expensive, take years to complete, and do not always give unequivocal results.

208. "Easing the Pain of Animal Tests." The Economist, v. 298, February 8, 1986, p. 82.

The U.S. Office of Technology Assessment report on alternatives (no. 229) suggests that scientists use fewer animals for LD50 tests, share control animals, use an animal as its own control in some drug tests, replace lovable animals with others, and replace animals with organs, cell cultures, or nonanimal tests.

209. "Fewer Test Animals Could Mean Safer Drugs." The Economist, v. 286, February 5, 1983, pp. 81-82.

An international committee reporting to the World Health Organisation recommends changes in the pre-market testing procedures for new drugs: reduce duplication of the same experiments in different countries; conduct earlier, limited testing on humans to find problems that animal tests might miss; reduce the numbers of animals used in LD50 tests; and monitor early signs of damage in laboratory animals.

210. "Good News for Rabbits! A Farewell to the Draize Test." Health, v. 15, November 1983, p. 14.

New tests, using cells from animals and membranes from chick eggs, are reliable without causing pain and can serve as alternatives to the Draize test for determining irritancy of cosmetics.

211. Holden, Constance. "New Focus on Replacing Animals in the Lab." Science, v. 215, January 1, 1982, pp. 35-38.

Specific alternatives to whole animal testing, particularly those using cell cultures and mathematical models, are described. The animal welfare movement and research scientists themselves are fostering the use of such alternatives. New methodologies open new areas of investigation which, in turn, lead to a reduction of animal use.

212. Kuker-Reines, Brandon. "Useless Animal Slaughter." Omni, v. 3, March 1981, p. 35.

Discusses the use of alternatives such as reasoning and mathematical modelling to replace animal experimentation. Inappropriate animal models are not necessarily applicable to human systems and their use often leads to unnecessary human experimentation.

63

213. National Research Council. Committee on Models for Biomedical Research. _Models for Biomedical Research: A New Perspective_. Washington, DC: National Academy Press, 1985. 180p.

The Committee recommends that support be given to good research, without taxonomic or phylogenetic bias, in order to expand the "matrix of biological knowledge." Although there is no adequate substitute for mammalian and even primate models in the study of many biomedical problems, other models (invertebrates, microorganisms, cell and tissue cultures, mathematical approaches) can contribute important information about living organisms, including humans.

214. "New Toxicity Test Could Cut Laboratory Deaths." _New Scientist_, v. 100, November 3, 1983, p. 328.

A new test, said to provide as much information as the LD50 test, is discussed. The new test uses half as many animals, enables most of the animals to survive, and provides more accurate and reproducible results.

215. Palca, Joseph. "Animal Welfare: OTA Squares Circle of Dissent." _Nature_, v. 319, February 6, 1986, p. 440.

Palca describes the comprehensive U.S. Office of Technology Assessment report (no. 229) on alternatives to animal use. Some animal welfare groups feel that the report, which says that some biological research will continue to require animals, does not reflect their views and is disappointing.

216. Pine, Devera. "World's Tiniest Test Animals." _Health_, v. 15, January 1983, p. 13.

Results of forty chemicals tested for toxicity on hydras, the lowest animals that still have tissues and organs, agreed completely with the results of "conventional" tests using higher animals.

217. "Policies on Animal Use in Research Studied." _Chemical & Engineering News_, v. 64, February 10, 1986, p. 23.

Describes the U.S. Office of Technology Assessment's report (no. 229) on alternatives to the use of animals in research, testing, and education as well as U.S. laws dealing with the use of laboratory animals.

218. Pratt, Dallas. <u>Alternatives to Pain in Experiments on Animals</u>, 2d. ed. New York: Argus Archives, 1980. 283p.
     Cites details of many painful experiments on animals and matches the experiments with proposed alternatives, drawn from new biomedical technologies, which would reduce animal suffering. Many of the experiments are criticized as being scientifically defective in addition to causing pain.

219. Reines, Brandon. "Animal Testing: New Controversy Over an Old Problem." <u>Family Health</u>, v. 12, March 1980, pp. 44-45.
     A case is made for funding the development of more effective, quicker, and less expensive testing methods than those that use animals. Certain drugs prove lethal to some animals yet are beneficial to humans, while the drug Thalidomide caused defects in human offspring but was "proven" safe in seven different animal species.

220. "Replacing Animals in Experiments." <u>USA Today</u>, v. 111, June 1983, pp. 9-10.
     Computers are used to replace animals in experiments conducted for educational purposes at the University of Texas Medical Branch.

221. "Research and Testing Without Animals." <u>Science News</u>, v. 128, August 24, 1985, p. 125.
     New tests to study eye injuries and infant botulism bacteria use cow eyes from slaughter houses and two rabbits rather than thousands of mice, respectively. The rabbit antibody test is faster, cheaper and more reliable than the older test.

222. "Routing Out Phylogenetic Bias." <u>Science News</u>, v. 127, May 18, 1985, p. 312.
     A National Academy of Sciences committee recommends that the National Institutes of Health stop favoring experiments on mammals and fund research on organisms not widely used at present. The committee admits, however, that other organisms and cell and tissue cultures cannot entirely replace intact mammals in research.

223. Rowan, Andrew N. "Test Tube Alternative: Outdated Toxicity Tests Waste Millions of Dollars and Animals' Lives and Should Be Replaced." The Sciences, v. 21, November 1981, pp. 16-19+.
      Argues for the development of alternative techniques which will either replace or reduce the numbers of animals used or refine tests so as to reduce distress. Describes tests presently in use and the problems involved in developing valid alternatives. Pressure from animal rights activists has prompted industrial funding of research, legislative efforts, and a government sponsored conference on the subject of alternatives.

224. "Scientific Progress Undermines Animal Experiments." New Scientist, v. 92, November 12, 1981, p. 420.
      A conference in London, devoted to progress in techniques which have led to significant decline in the use of laboratory animals, had scientists discussing such alternatives as the use of bioengineering techniques for vaccine production and human placenta to assay drug effectiveness.

225. Smyth, D. H. Alternatives to Animal Experiments. London: Scholar Press, 1978. 218p.
      Techniques such as chromatography, mass spectrometry, radioimmunoassay, and use of isotopes are employed as alternatives to reduce or eliminate the use of animals in biomedical research. A discussion of why alternatives are not more widely used follows descriptions of particular animal experiments.

226. Sun, Marjorie. "Animal Welfare Bills on Legislative Agenda." Science, v. 219, February 25, 1983, p. 939.
      Bills likely to be introduced in Congress would mandate and/or encourage the search for and use of alternatives such as mathematical modelling and tissue culture. A National Research Council report (no. 213) touts progress in the use of microorganisms and cell culture for mutagen testing.

227. "Three R's." <u>Scientific American</u>, v. 254, April 1986, pp. 68-70.

The U.S. Office of Technology Assessment has issued a report (no. **229**) which calls for the development of alternatives to animal experimentation as presently practiced. Feasible alternatives are categorized as the "three R's:" replacement with nonanimals, reduction in the number of animals used, and refinement of techniques to reduce pain and distress.

228. U.S. Congress. House of Representatives. Committee on Science and Technology. Subcommittee on Science, Research and Technology. <u>Alternatives to Animal Use in Research and Testing</u>. Washington, DC: Government Printing Office, 1986. Superintendent of Documents number Y4.Sci2:99/130.

Government officials testified as to what the federal government is doing to develop and implement research methods that may not use animals, use fewer animals, or cause less pain. Also testifying was the director of the Johns Hopkins Center for Alternatives to Animal Testing.

229. U.S. Office of Technology Assessment. <u>Alternatives to Animal Use in Research, Testing, and Education</u>. Washington, DC: Government Printing Office, February 1986. Superintendent of Documents number Y3.T22/2:2Ai5.

This document tells how animals are used in research, testing, and education and describes alternatives including reduction of animal use, use of other living systems, computer simulations, and the use of existing information. Ethical, funding, and legislative considerations are also discussed. Appendices list guidelines, regulations, accredited laboratory animals facilities, international agreements, and a glossary. A summary report, Y3.T22/2:2Ai5/sum, is also available from the GPO.

230. Vines, Gail. "Animal Deaths Are Unnecessary, Say Experimenters." <u>New Scientist</u>, v. 96, November 4, 1982, p. 275.

British scientists report the numbers of animals used in toxicology testing could be significantly reduced with the use of alternatives such as tissue culture, elimination of the LD50 test, pooling of test results within industry, and more research in humans.

231. Walton, Susan. "Choosing More Models for Biomedical Research." BioScience, v. 35, July/August 1985, pp. 406-407.

Reports on a National Research Council report (no. 213) which encourages researchers to use many organisms, particularly those that have been widely studied, to build a "matrix of biological knowledge." Research on a single species, particularly a mammal, is discouraged.

232. **Walton, Susan. "Congress Puts Bioassay to the Test." BioScience, v. 31, April 1981, pp. 287-290.**

Describes proposed legislation which would encourage development of alternative testing methods and a three day conference, requested by Congress, to discuss toxic substance testing and regulation. The role of chimpanzees, which are very similar to humans, is described. The practical goal is to reduce the use of animals whenever possible. Total elimination is not considered feasible.

Industry's Role in Developing Alternatives to Animal Experimentation

233. Dagani, Ron. "Alternative Methods Could Cut Animal Use in Toxicity Tests." <u>Chemical & Engineering News</u>, v. 61, October 31, 1983, pp. 7-13.

   Motivated by the animal welfare movement and the shortcomings inherent in animal research, researchers are developing alternative tests and research techniques with funds provided by industry. Specific new tests to assess eye irritation and chemical toxicity are described.

234. Dagani, Ron. "In-Vitro Methods May Offer Alternatives to Animal Testing." <u>Chemical & Engineering News</u>, v. 62, November 12, 1984, pp. 25-28.

   Experiments designed to develop alternatives to the use of live animals in research and testing have been funded by the Johns Hopkins Center for Alternatives to Animal Testing, an organization which receives much of its money from industry. Advantages of in-vitro testing and some of the specific experiments are described.

235. Davis, Donald A. "Great Expectations." <u>Drug & Cosmetic Industry</u>, v. 128, June 1981, p. 35.

   The current "scatter-shot" approach, whereby industry and government fund many research programs, will not be effective in developing alternatives to traditional testing approaches. Animal protectionists will feel "duped" when the money runs out and there is still not an in-vitro alternative to the Draize test.

236. Davis, Donald A. "Is There an Alternative?" <u>Drug & Cosmetic Industry</u>, v. 133, July 1983, p. 23.

   An editorial stating that animal protectionist tactics have forced industry to fund expensive research into alternatives, pressured Congress to consider legislation to curb animal testing abuses, and fostered the illusion that industry could conduct its business without the use of test animals. It is a sham to think that assurance of product safety can be achieved without animal testing.

237. Davis, Donald A. "Too Passive a Defense." Drug & Cosmetic Industry, v. 134, February 1984, p. 31.
Industry should use reasoned, logical arguments and carefully selected examples to make the case in favor of animal testing. The animal protectionists are having such success in raiding laboratories and getting laws passed because industry and trade associations lack an organized response.

238. "Johns Hopkins Is Selected as Site for Center for Animal Test Alternatives." Drug & Cosmetic Industry, v. 129, November 1981, p. 42+.
In response to criticism from animal protection groups, the Cosmetic, Toiletry & Fragrance Association chose Johns Hopkins School of Hygiene and Public Health to establish a research center for developing alternatives to the use of animals in cosmetic testing. Although some animal tests will still be necessary, the need will be significantly reduced by the research conducted at the Center for Animal Test Alternatives.

239. "Progress in Nonanimal Cosmetic Irritancy Test." Chemical & Engineering News, v. 60, October 11, 1982, pp. 7-8.
Two Rockefeller University scientists are correlating results of Draize tests with results obtained by studying the effects of suspected irritant chemicals on certain properties of cell cultures. The results correlate positively and could lead to the development of a test system which predicts irritancy without using live rabbits.

240. "Revlon Project Shows Promise for Draize Test Alternative." Drug & Cosmetic Industry, v. 133, July 1983, pp. 44+.
Rockefeller University scientists, funded by Revlon, are developing four in-vitro assays which could replace the Draize test with the use of cell culture techniques. Specifics of the work are described.

241. Richards, Robin. "Animal Test Alternatives: A Status Report on What's Happeing." Drug & Cosmetic Industry, v. 132, April 1983, pp. 30-32+.
Public pressure and the high cost of animal research has prompted the industry to fund research into alternatives to the Draize and other tests. Revlon gave $750,000 for four projects and the Cosmetic, Toiletry & Fragrance Association, led by Avon and Bristol-Myers, set up the Center for Alternatives to Animal Testing at Johns Hopkins. Work at the Center is described.

242. Richards, Robin. "A Status Report on Animal Test Alternatives." Drug & Cosmetic Industry, v. 132, May 1983, pp. 42-46+.
Pharmaceutical and cosmetic companies are reducing animal use by using alternative testing methods such as a modified LD50, in-vitro tests, chromatography, pyrogen tests, modified Draize eye tests, and enzyme tests. The companies are funding research at Johns Hopkins and Rockefeller Universities to further develop alternatives.

243. "Search for Painless Toxicity Testing." New Scientist, v. 94, May 20, 1982, p. 476.
Coordinated by the Fund for the Replacement of Animals in Medical Science, five chemical and cosmetic companies are funding trials to test the safety of chemicals without using animals.

244. Smith, R. Jeffrey. "Revlon Funds Animal Test Research." Science, v. 211, January 16, 1981, p. 260.
In the midst of a consumer boycott and letter writing campaign, Revlon, Inc., the major cosmetics company, announced a grant of $750,000 to be spent at Rockefeller University on research to find alternatives to the Draize test.

245. Starr, Douglas. "Good News for Lab Animals." Omni, v. 4, July 1982, p. 35.
Alternatives are being developed, with funds provided by industry, to eliminate painful animal experiments such as Draize testing of chemicals on rabbits' eyes.

71

Author Index

Godlovitch, S.: 139.
Goodman, W.: 12.
Greenberg, G.: 130.
Hager, M.: 6.
Harris, J.: 139.
Heneson, N.: 131, 185.
Henig, R. M.: 150.
Herbert, W.: 104, 186, 187.
Herscovici, A.: 13.
Herzog, H. A.: 35.
Hines, C.: 71.
Hoff, C.: 41.
Holden, C.: 14, 78, 151, 165, 188-191, 211.
Hollands, C.: 117.
Igelsrud, D.: 152.
Inglehart, J. K.: 79.
James, C.: 132.
Jamieson, D.: 42.
Jones, P. M.: 15.
Katz, S.: 6.
Keehn, J. D.: 62.
Kehrer, D.: 193.
Kelly, J. A.: 43.
King, F. A.: 44, 145.
Kuker-Reines, B.: 212.
Lauer, M.: 166, 167.
Lauter, D.: 194.
Leccese, M.: 133.
Leepson, M.: 16.
Lewis, P. B.: 80.
Linden, E.: 146.
Lubinska, A.: 119.
Lutes, C.: 34.
MacKenzie, D.: 120, 121.
Maddox, J.: 45.
Magel, C. R.: 1, 2.
Mayer, W. V.: 153.
Mayo, D. G.: 134.
McDonald, K. L.: 81.
McGiffin, H.: 154.
McKay, S.: 122.
Miller, H. B.: 134.
Miller, J. A.: 82, 195.
Mishkin, B.: 83.
Moss, T. H.: 84.
Neffe, J.: 123.
Nevin, D.: 168.
Noah, T.: 197.